A Pathway through the Sky

by James A. McLaughry

with David Allen

ISBN-13: 978-1517484583
ISBN-10: 1517484588

TABLE OF CONTENTS

Prologue	*August 24th, 1944*	1
Chapter 1	*Beginnings*	11
Chapter 2	*Off to the War*	18
Chapter 3	*Our First Mission*	26
Chapter 4	*Skies of Fire and Death*	33
Chapter 5	*The Voice of God in Combat*	41
Chapter 6	*A New Mission in Life*	48
Chapter 7	*Reaching Out*	55
Chapter 8	*Assignment to USSTAF*	65
Chapter 9	*Personal Pilot for a General*	76
Chapter 10	*Trip Through the Land of the Dead*	84
Chapter 11	*Is There an Answer to War?*	92
Chapter 12	*Returning Home*	99
Chapter 13	*Physician to a World Diseased*	106
Chapter 14	*A Light in the Sky*	110
Chapter 15	*A Pathway through a Storm*	115
Chapter 16	*August 1957 - Reflections*	122
Epilogue	*James A. McLaughry – 1924-2015*	126
Afterword	*Background Information*	128

First Lieutenant, James A. McLaughry, USSAF
London, England - November, 1944

PROLOGUE
August 24th, 1944

It was zero hour.

In the early morning light, I could see the dark phantom forms of the B-24s warming up on the perimeter track. The first rays of dawn were struggling through a low overcast in the east and a chill wind was blowing in from the North Sea. One by one, bombers in our squadron were moving around the track behind the lead plane.

I cast my eye over the dozens of gauges, meters and flying instruments in front of me, shining like so many cold eyes from the darkness. Long before this moment, the armorers had loaded the heavy bombs into the bay. Mechanics and ground-crew chiefs had checked every detail and warmed the engines. All was in running order, the thousands of moving parts, all the veins and arteries of this steel giant that was to lift us into the air and carry us on to target.

There was much to put one's mind to in the minutes before take-off. I ran through the check list again in my mind. It helped to fight off the clutching fear and tensions that knotted my insides.

I glanced at Oats, the first pilot, on my left. Not many words passed between us in these moments. Silence seemed to express best what we were feeling in our hearts and stomachs. His eyes were fixed on the line of planes ahead of us. Slowly we moved into position.

The second hand on my wrist-watch ticked relentlessly on.

I looked out across the field through the tears of moisture on the windshield. Down the black tarmac runway, I could make out the giant clump of trees at the crossing of the landing strips, silhouetted against the glow in the eastern sky. A white vapor rose in curls from the dank fields nearby.

Now was the moment!

The signal came. The lead plane roared down the runway,

Prologue – August 24th, 1944

momentarily lost in the darkness of the pre-dawn. Then it was seen again, rising over the dark line of the English country-side, climbing into the dullness of the sky, spectacular in its flight. Now the number two plane sped away. One by one the bombers on the track moved up behind. Every thirty seconds the next plane in line thundered off into the air, into the unknown perils of the day.

We turned into position. The runway stretched away before us. I pushed the throttles down and the plane roared to life, all four engines snarling in satanic fury. White bursts of flame leapt from the exhausts. Painfully slowly, we began to move, picking up speed gradually down the strip. Power surged through the whole aircraft, the pulse of its giant heart racing to a fever pitch. Faster and faster we fled, every muscle taut and strained. Objects on either side of the runway flashed past us in the early morning light.

I glanced at the air-speed indicator. These were anxious moments; we were at maximum weight, carrying a full bomb load and 2,600 gallons of gasoline aboard. Slowly Oats eased back on the stick, the whole frame of the plane shuddering and shaking until the last few feet of the runway. With a burst of energy, we staggered over the hedge at the end and lifted out across the trees. We rose up slowly through the cold veil of fog rolling in from the sea.

The wheels came up into the wells and we slacked back our throttles, shifting into regular climbing power. Beneath the wing I could see the macadam roads and hedges, the patchwork of fields here and there covered by a white mist.

We headed out over the Wash, rising steadily. The crinkled face of the sea, touched with rolling white-caps, stretched out to the distance. To the east, the sky was reddening to herald the sun.

We climbed steadily to 8,000 feet. At the end of the second stages of the climb, we banked over, turning 180 degrees in our course, back towards the field. All up and down the coast of England, thousands of other bombers were also in flight, circling into formations, into giant wings, to fly together over the continent. We could see hundreds of aircraft at various altitudes, forming into the different groups.

A Pathway through the Sky

There was our field below us now. The runways seemed strangely foreshortened from this height. I could see the large clump of trees at the runway crossing which so clearly marked our field from the rest.

We closed in behind the plane we were to follow in our squadron formation.

... It was getting difficult to breathe. The altimeter needle pointed to 12,000 feet. I pulled on my oxygen mask.

We moved out over the North Sea, thousands of planes – an air armada moving majestically across the skies of morning. The sun rose out of a bleary pillow of clouds and cast a challenging eye at us as we rose on upwards over the continent.

There was a solid undercast today. Our navigator was busy at the radar instruments, tracking our course. ... Oats gave the order for the tail turret gunner to test-fire his guns. There was a brief deafening chatter as the fifty-calibers blazed away into space. The tail gunner called in his "Okay!" All was well on the waist turret. The nose turret checked in. All in order. The guns were ready.

An hour passed. The sun drew up into the sky, shining brilliantly down on the turbulent contours of the cloud cover. Wispy silver strands of cirrus were flung high across the blue world above us. The altimeter showed 21,000 feet. Oats turned over the controls to me.

Time passed slowly. There were many details to care for in the course of our flight over the continent.

By 0945 hours, we were over the Rhine River and crossing the border from France into Germany. Now and then through a clearing in the cloud cover, I caught glimpses of the German landscape – the melancholy green of the rain-soaked countryside, a narrow road, a solitary farmhouse. A cheerless glimpse – then, more clouds.

Somewhere down there was our target for today. It was some factory in the south of Germany. I imagined its smokestacks standing stark against the sky, gigantic structures shining wet in the rain, the hiss of steam, the swearing thunder of heavy machinery, the

Prologue – August 24th, 1944

shimmering orange glow of the furnaces. It was one of the vital engines of a nation at war – at war against us – a war whose outcome depended on efficiency and production and turn-out.

It had to be destroyed. We must level it to the ground in a direct hit. It was the only way. This was the story of war – a war to which I was committed with my very life. We had to kill to save lives. We had to destroy. We had to be cruel, savage and brutal before we could win the peace.

Bursts of flak began to come up all around us, little black bursts, then a ball of fire and deadly splintering steel – then a purple smudge of smoke left hanging in the sky. I watched the flak bursts beginning to make their marks on all sides - big tracks near a large group of planes, sometimes directly ahead, in line with our own group.

Suddenly, and without warning, there was a tremendous impact on our aircraft. The plane lurched crazily upward. Our Number One engine, the outboard port engine, had been hit. A fire started.

"Feather Number One, Mac! On the double," yelled Oats.

I pounced on the feathering button. Flames were leaping around the mount. I cut the ignition and the propellers slowed and locked into the wind, inert. ... Gradually the wind began to take effect and the fire died down and went out.

This setback in power caused us to drop slightly out of formation. By the time we reached the target area, we were lagging behind the plane in front of us by about four or five hundred yards.

We turned into the bomb run, and at the given word, dropped our load. It was a race against time to get out of the area as quickly as possible – the flak was coming up thick and fast. Our squadron banked off to the starboard beam and turned towards home.

Then we were hit again. A piece of shrapnel from an air burst ripped into the oil line of our Number Three engine, our starboard inboard engine. A solid black stream of oil flowed instantly from the leak out over the back tail fin. Our navigation instruments and radar were knocked out in the same blast.

We were unable to keep up with the formation and fell steadily behind the planes in our group, losing altitude gradually. Within ten or twelve minutes, we could no longer see the bombers in our squadron ahead of us.

Had we known at that moment how serious our plight was, we would surely have turned north to Sweden or else landed in nearby Switzerland. As it was, we were unaware of the dangers in chancing the flight home. We continued on alone.

We flew for some length of time without incident, going down steadily. The events of the previous minutes had happened with terrible swiftness and only now did we begin to fully grasp our plight. We were utterly unprotected. With one engine dead and another, losing oil rapidly, there was no telling how long we'd be able to fly.

By about 1330 hours it became obvious to me that we were going to have serious trouble with our Number Three engine. The pressure in the oil line had already dropped to approximately forty pounds from the normal of seventy. Every minute it dropped further and further. In our training we had been taught that, no matter how severe the emergency, we were to feather the engine at thirty pounds pressure on the Liberator bomber. If the pressure dropped below that level, we'd be deprived of any further chance to do so.

We faced two alternatives. If we did feather our Number Three, we would no longer be able to keep up the airspeed necessary to maintain altitude. We would have to crash-land, probably in the North Sea. Our two good engines could not muster enough power to keep us going.

If we went against all our training and did *not* feather the engine, we would be in serious danger of eventually flying out of control. The oil would run dry after an hour or more. The pistons would seize in the scorching heat. The propeller might windmill at high speeds, creating violent vibrations, possibly shaking the engine from its mount. In either case, we would most probably have to ditch our

Prologue – August 24th, 1944

plane on the open waters of the sea.

Through clear patches in the cloud cover, I could now see the restless gray waters of the North Sea. We could survive for fifteen minutes in those icy waves, maybe less. Whatever way the plot developed, whatever means that fate devised, it seemed that only a miracle could get us back to England now.

As it became increasingly clear that we were in for an open-sea ditching, I grew very afraid. It was a cold fear, a dull pain gnawing away and knotting up my insides. It was the terrible uncertainty of not knowing what death was like or how it would come. I had lost all confidence in myself. This was a situation beyond my control, something bigger than I could handle. If I ever had any of a hero's courage, it completely failed me at this point.

Years before this moment, I had met people who had told me about God as a guiding force in their everyday life. They had given their lives to following His will. Their direction came, they said, from the definite accurate information that could come from the Mind of God to the mind of man.

They had challenged me to accept God's plan for my life – and to help build a new world.

Could He, at this very moment, give me the "definite accurate information" needed to save our lives?

I was ready to believe and to listen.

At 1410 hours, the pressure level in the Number Three oil line hit thirty pounds. It was time to feather. We had made preliminary preparations for an emergency ditching. From the cockpit, I sensed the unspoken fears and panic in the crew, and in Oats.

I prayed and put my thumb on the button.

Instantly, I was filled with a penetrating sense of warning. The word exploded three times in my mind: *"No! No! No!"* I felt compelled to obey, even though it went against all my training and better judgment. Perhaps it was the answer to my prayer.

I dropped my hand. If this was indeed God's guidance, I was going to put all my trust in it, whatever happened.

The engineer, who had more training than I, argued vociferously. But I remained firm. Never had a thought come so clearly or with such strength to me. I refused to feather the engine.

Humanly, it might look like an insanely wild decision, taken in moments of confusion and panic. We were running a terrific risk by not feathering our Number Three. Anything could happen. But at least we were still flying. Perhaps we could hold out for even an hour longer. There might still be a slim chance of getting home – that is, if we could maintain flying altitude. We might just make it.

Oats accepted my decision.

We flew on. Time dragged. Though we had stretched our descent out as much as possible, we were now at about 2,000 feet above the water, flying deep in the North Sea fog by compass alone. A half hour passed - maybe more. I lost my sense of time.

In spite of the mounting peril we faced, I felt a new strength coming into me, a strength that was not my own. By one simple step of implicit obedience, I had put myself under a new Authority. I had entrusted every action wholly to God.

I began to think of an old Bible verse I had once memorized: "I am with you, even unto the ends of the world."

Oats reached up for his crash harness to prepare for an open-sea ditching and gave the wheel to the engineer for the moment. I kept my attention riveted on the instrument panel.

Suddenly, I was prompted by some inner feeling to turn and look out of the starboard window. To my horror, I saw a B-24 lumbering blindly through the fog on a direct collision course with us.

I grabbed the wheel, yanking back with all my might. There was a

Prologue – August 24th, 1944

crazy lurch as we nosed up into the air. The other bomber roared thunderously underneath our wing, missing us by a few feet. It was terrifyingly close. Oats spun around in time to catch sight of it as it flew into the distance and disappeared into the fog.

We were completely stunned and shattered by the sudden shock – it almost had a paralyzing effect. It happened so quickly. The near-collision fairly well destroyed the last shred of confidence and calm in the crew. If there had been any hope in them, it had gone – totally gone by now. They had given up.

With every minute, our danger increased. Of that, no one was more fully aware than I. We could not tell how many more minutes we could keep on flying. The oil pressure was steadily dropping. We were constantly losing altitude and there was no sight of land. Very few bomber crews had ever survived a ditching in the North Sea. It would take a few more miracles to get us home.

At 1525 hours I realized that we could keep flying for approximately fifteen minutes longer – twenty minutes at the most. There was still no sight of land. Despair began to creep into my heart too.

I was almost ready to give up when we first sighted the coastline through the haze – just a jagged rocky shore, flailed by the crashing breakers up and down its length. Seconds later we crossed over it, flying at an altitude of 800 feet. Spread out beneath us was England – England at last! – England we had thought we might never see again. I praised God from a full heart.

Our immediate problem was to find a place to land. The navigator was busily trying to locate us over the maze of country roads and railway lines and forests and fields ... but in vain. It was impossible to get perspective of the area from our low altitude. Details passed so quickly beneath us.

The minutes were running out. We couldn't hold out much longer ... every moment was precious.

Incredibly, a few more minutes later we flew right over our own base. It was unmistakable; there was the big clump of trees at the crossing of the runways, the tower, our own barracks area! I was overwhelmed with joy. *We were going to make it!*

We quickly and without further incident, turned, came in and landed on the runway.

For some reason, none of us in the crew felt like shouting ... or even speaking. What had happened had been a deeper experience for us than that. It was something more than could be accredited to courage or the intelligent action of any individual.

It had been a miracle – a miracle mission. God had led us back home, every last step of the way.

I walked down from the debriefing room with Oats to the bicycle stand outside the building. A gentle rain was falling. At the bottom of the stairs, we met Bill Drummond, our engineer, and fell into conversation with him.

Bill had been checking over our Number Three engine with the ground-crew chief. There had been a few meager drops of oil left in the Number Three oil line, not nearly enough to keep the engine going. The engine would have continued to function, he told us, for about a minute and a half longer – at the most three minutes. After that? Well, there was no telling what might have happened.

At supper that night, I chatted with George Judd, our navigator, as we stood in line for our food. Our navigation and radar instruments had been shot out in the second flak burst. George had immediately set us on an estimated course for England, reckoning by compass alone to get us back to our base, through the fog and over the trackless sea. He had traced that course on his maps before supper. We had been heading in the wrong direction, about three or four degrees north of East Anglia. We would have missed that bulge in the eastern coast altogether had it not been for the near mid-air collision in the North Sea. In swerving away from the other B-24, he discovered we had altered course by about six or seven degrees to the

Prologue – August 24th, 1944

southwest, thus bringing us in over East Anglia, and eventually *right to our own base!*

Had it not been for that near-accident, we would have flown over the open water for another twenty-five minutes before crossing the coast of England ...

We had been at the mercy of our own quick decisions all day. One wrong reaction could have spelled awful death for a whole crew. But this day something delivered us from disaster - something bigger than our own decisions or actions.

... Something so amazing, so miraculous that it could only be God – the Voice of God in combat calling us.

CHAPTER 1
Beginnings

My home, New Wilmington, lies nestled in a valley among the low rolling hills of western Pennsylvania, not far from the great industrial city of Pittsburgh. It is a small town, peaceful and quiet, and away from the main highways and traffic arteries of the state.

Long years ago our McLaughry ancestors came across the seas from Scotland and Ireland and landed in the New World. They soon spread out to the West, across the farming country of Pennsylvania and Ohio, and beyond to the Great Plains. My great-grandfather helped to found the lovely college of Westminster in our town of New Wilmington. The stately college chapel stands sentinel by the village green, the bells from its gothic tower pealing away the passing hours.

Dad was a tool manufacturer and, at the time, operated the only industry in New Wilmington, employing about 18 men. He realized, I suppose, when he built the factory, that our town was an unlikely spot for economic success. But he had grown up in the country, away from the rush and traffic of the big cities. He wanted his children to grow up in the country as well.

My mother was an accomplished concert pianist and had earned a Master's degree in French at Ohio State University. Mom and Dad got married and settled down in New Wilmington on top of the hill in a lovely house with walls of rough-hewn stone which Dad designed and helped build. They named it "Stone Gables".

We were a family of six. My sister Beth was three years older than I. Bill, my brother, is six years younger than I. My youngest sister, Peggy, was born the year I graduated from high school.

As a young boy, I used to work at my Aunt Bessie's sanatorium, "The Overlook", mowing lawns, trimming hedges and washing windows. Aunt Bessie was one of the leading physicians in Pennsylvania – among the first women doctors.

During summer days, we would often go as a family to visit my grandparents who lived about a hundred miles to the north near Lake Chautauqua. They owned a small cottage on the shores of the lake. Many were the wonderful happy days that we spent splashing about in the water and rambling along the rocks in our bare feet in the summer sun. They were warm, joyful days, and we were young.

In the winters, the solemn skies brought the ice and snow to our hills. White drifts would pile high before our window and all the way down the street. Many cold wintery days, we would ski down the hill to school on the fresh snow – it was too deep to bring the old car out of the garage. We loved best of all the blizzards which brought the deepest of snows. School would likely be called off for the day. Somehow those were happier holidays than all the rest.

In this peaceful rural community, we grew up as a family and together went through the dramas, the hopes, the fears, the sunshine and shadows of our different lives. Beth went on to college. Mother began to teach classes in French at the same time. And in late August of 1939, I went back to high school as a senior.

Only a few days after school had started, the war broke out.

How well I remember that first day of war! We were in our high school classroom. The principal brought in a radio for us. It was awful news: Hitler had invaded Poland. We could hear Neville Chamberlain, Prime Minister of Great Britain, broadcasting from London:

> *"This morning, the British Ambassador in Berlin handed to the German government a final note, stating that unless we heard from them by eleven o'clock that they were preparing at once to withdraw their troops from Poland, a state of war would exist between us. I have to tell you that no such undertaking has been received, and, in consequence, this country is at war with Germany."*

It had started. World War II had started over the seas in faraway Europe ... a dreadful war in which I myself would one day play a part.

A Pathway through the Sky

And yet, Europe was thousands of miles away, far beyond the green rolling hills where we lived our lives. Perhaps in Pittsburgh, the mighty industries were being mobilized into the war effort to build tanks and planes and guns. Perhaps a few Navy pilots buzzed their planes over our quiet town – pilots who had gone to college in New Wilmington, men who had grown up in our area. Perhaps the newspapers were full of the horrors of the war. But somehow it was very remote from us, remote from our lives, our careers, our families.

I graduated from high school the following summer and entered college at the age of sixteen. With all the hope and ambition of youth, I threw myself into various courses, preparing myself for a life in politics. Politically I sided with the working people, the farmers, the less wealthy in college, and championed them as opposed to the smaller group of those higher in the social scale. I did the best I could to equip myself with experience in leadership.

One Sunday evening in December, 1941, I was walking to a meeting of the Young People's Christian Union. A friend shouted to me from across the street. *Pearl Harbor has been invaded!* The Japanese had attacked the American fleet by surprise.

Within days, America was at war with all three Axis powers.

We were in it now – right up to the neck. *We* were at war! The waiting and the watching were at last over. As I continued down the street in the twilight, it seemed incredible, almost too hard to believe.

Eighty years before, our great grandfathers and great granduncles had grabbed their pitchforks from the wall and had jumped aboard the train for Gettysburg to defend it against the Confederate troops under Lee, advancing from the south. Now, again, we were called to defend our homeland.

I enlisted in the United States Army Air Corps in October 1942 and was called into the service the next February. During the early months of 1943, I underwent the first stages of my training in Kent, Ohio, and in Miami Beach, Florida.

Beginnings

Spring turned into summer. The weather warmed and the trees came bursting joyously into life. In the warmth of the long afternoons, I began thinking of the vast blue expanses of the sky, windswept, cruel and fascinating – the cold realms I was soon to enter as a flying man. Since boyhood I had longed to fly. Every time I had seen a plane soaring on high, I had dearly wanted to become a pilot. Now at last it began to look as though my fondest hopes were beginning to materialize.

In June, we moved to San Antonio, Texas for further training. We boarded the train in Ohio and for 30 hours sped across the country, traveling deeper and deeper into the south. What country it was - the flat open spaces of Texas, the sand underfoot, the sun blazing like a dry furnace in the sky. The Texas summer was scorching.

2nd Lt. James McLaughry
US Army Air Corps 1943

San Antonio was the home of Kelly Field and Randolph Field, vast Army Air Corps bases where thousands of men were finally allocated as bombardiers, navigators and pilots. During the next weeks, we were given tests of a very exacting nature, psychological tests and intelligence tests, psycho-motor tests, tests of endurance and of emotional stability under strain. Our habits, our weaknesses, our tendencies under emergency conditions were reviewed with acute detail and thoroughness.

In August, I was sent for training in the pre-flight school in San Antonio for further study in aircraft identification, in signals communication and the Morse code, and in the elementary fundamentals of navigation. It was a nine-week course.

Summer passed. Autumn blew in across the vast open spaces of Texas. The high winds flung dramatic cirrus formations across the world above us and blood-red sunsets majestically framed the evening skies. I had never seen such striking sunsets in my life. The nights were silent, chill and crystal clear, the stars shining cold and brilliant overhead.

With the return of autumn, the Allied Forces overseas were working their way up the boot of Italy in some of the bloodiest fighting of the war. The summer had seen, in many ways, the turning of the tide in Europe. Sicily had been invaded. The Axis powers had been put on the defensive. Now that the Allied Forces were once again on the continent of Europe, Hitler was threatened more than he had been since the outbreak of war.

Meanwhile, the U.S. Eighth and Ninth Air Forces were building up at a stupendous rate in an effort to knock out vital industries and refineries in the heart of Germany. On August 1st, there had been a low-level bombing attack on the Ploesti oil refineries in Rumania, one of Hitler's most precious sources of aviation fuel. Air power, it seemed, would be pivotal in the next crucial months of the war.

A flying man can never forget the experience of his first solo flight. The day stands out vividly in my mind; it was an October afternoon. I had been flying with my instructor in a PT-19, landing and taking off from a small field several miles out of Muskogee, Oklahoma. About the middle of the afternoon, after several circuits, we landed and taxied over to the edge of the field. The instructor turned off the engine.

"Okay Mac. You take it now." He leapt down to the ground.

I taxied slowly over to the end of the field, and pushed forward on the throttle. The little plane quickly gathered speed and raced down the runway, lift coming into the wings. Gently I eased back on the stick and the plane lifted up into the air. I climbed steadily to about 800 feet and banked back towards the field. The vast amber plains of Oklahoma spread out beneath me on every side, reaching on to the deep blue of the horizon.

Beginnings

After a few circuits, I turned back over the field, dropped down gradually and came in for my approach. I landed quite easily and pulled in, bringing the plane over to the edge of the field. In my heart, I felt a feeling of joy and accomplishment. A boyhood dream had come true! I was a pilot!

My flight training continued all that autumn. I got thoroughly accustomed to the small PT-19 with its single low wing and open-air cockpits, the wild flights with the raw wind lashing against the exposed parts of my face. It was a real pleasure to fly.

During the winter and early months of 1944, I started training in a twin-engine Cessna, the old AT-17. It was built with a wooden frame covered in fabric. In advanced flying school, we called it "the bamboo bomber". It was in this plane that we were trained in formation flying in preparation for bomber squadrons.

One adventure during this period stands out vividly in my mind.

We were flying one night in a tight formation of three aircraft. I was on the left wing of the instructor's plane. It was pitch dark. Suddenly my starboard engine coughed to a stop. My plane swung in towards the instructor's plane due to the power loss on my starboard side. I missed his empennage with a few feet to spare.

Immediately I got on the radio. My engine had stopped! What was I to do? Had I tried carburetor heat? Perhaps my engine was icing. Yes, I had tried that. It didn't work.

I was dropping back considerably due to the loss of power. Soon I was alone out in the middle of the pitch blackness of Texas. I didn't know where I was.

My co-pilot started to get panicky. I noticed him undoing his seat belt and moving towards the door in order to bail out. With my right arm, I pushed him hard on his chest, throwing him back into his seat. He quickly came to his senses and began to calm down.

A Pathway through the Sky

"Cut the gas supply to the number two engine," I shouted. At least we could prevent the danger of a fire.

In the distance now, I could just make out the lights of our base. We might be able to make it back. I called the control tower and got them to clear the planes off the field. Stretching out our descent, we came in slowly on one engine, losing altitude steadily until we got to the field. Quickly we came down. We landed safely, both of us greatly relieved to get back on the ground.

Our instructors lost no time, however, but gave us another plane and sent us up immediately again that night.

... My flying adventures were starting early

As a new US Army Air Corps pilot, Jim McLaughry returns on leave to visit his family in 1943. Seated left to right: his younger brother Bill, his older sister Beth, his mother Mary Margaret, his youngest sister Peggy, and his father, Jim Sr.

Chapter 2

Off to the War

After graduating from advanced flying school in the spring of 1944, I was assigned as a co-pilot on a B-24. In Salt Lake City, I met the crew I was to fly with. These were men I would get to know very well in the next months over Europe, men with whom I would go through hell and high water in the skies over Germany and France. It was the beginning of friendships that lasted not only through the war, but down through the years after the war ended.

Otho Summers from New York City was my first pilot, a wonderful, friendly, good-natured guy. He immediately invited me to call him by his nickname, "Oats". His father was the president of an insurance company and Oats, himself, had grown up in the center of New York society life.

George Judd, hailing from upstate New York, became our navigator. George was reliable and steady, and later turned out to be one of the best navigators in our bomber squadron in combat overseas.

Bill Drummond was our engineer and top turret gunner, a quiet fellow, efficient and dependable. "Punch" O'Kane, a fellow Pennsylvanian, became our tough hard-hitting waist gunner and the armorer of the plane. Our other waist gunner was Bill Flesey from Jersey City, a big blond boy with an infectious sense of humor and a real knack for making friends. Our bombardier, Henry Streicher, was jovial and fierce, a man of roaring exuberance, always getting into impossible predicaments.

Jimmy "Daddy" Fender from Valdosta, Georgia, was the only southerner in our crew. He became our radio operator. He was a quiet, well-mannered, very clear-thinking fellow. We quickly became friends.

Late in May, 1944, we went to Lincoln, Nebraska to get various items of equipment and to go through medical tests and inoculations prior to our flight across to Europe. We were thoroughly checked out for about ten days in a brand new B-24 Liberator which we, as a crew, were to fly over to Great Britain on our way to combat.

The Lincoln air base was a major field for the dispersal of planes and crews for Europe and overseas. For security reasons, the Air Force took precautions to obscure the tail numbers of aircraft that were sent out. Daily the big bombers could be heard thundering off during very early hours of the morning.

One night in June, only a few days after D-Day, our turn came.

We were headed first for Westover, Massachusetts and beyond that, across the North Atlantic to Scotland and England as a part of the U.S. Eighth Air Force Bomber Command.

Our route from Lincoln to Westover took us within 60 miles of my home, New Wilmington, Pennsylvania. We decided to deflect from our course and go buzz the town a couple of times on our way. This diversion was completely unchecked with the United States Army Air Corps, but the crew were enthusiastic about the idea. We proceeded south from our course in the approximate direction of the town.

I wrote a note to Mom and Dad and stuffed it in a pillow case with some Coca Cola bottle tops, Salt Lake City street-car tokens, old bread crusts and a fifty cent piece. I enclosed a list of the addresses of the rest of the crew and asked Mom to write to their families. We would make a "drop", right over the park in the heart of town.

We were approaching my home country now. Down below were the rolling hills and farmlands of western Pennsylvania. A slight mist was locked in the valleys and rising. It was ten o'clock on a fine morning – a perfect Saturday morning. I couldn't help feeling homesick.

Oats gave me the controls and I brought the plane down to about 300 feet. George Judd was busy trying to locate our position on the map. "Mac", he yelled, "does New Wilmington have any big landmark in it, a tower or something?"

"Yes, a big square tower, the Westminster College tower. It's right in the center of town." The tower on campus would be unmistakable from the air.

We had to be getting very close now. Yet, somehow, nothing looked familiar to me. Were things so different from the air?

"That should be it over there, Mac," Judd shouted.

There was a town in the distance with a tall tower. I headed for it and minutes later came roaring in over the roof-tops. But this was not New Wilmington! With some difficulty I recognized the town as Mercer, about nine miles away from home. Judd had seen the tower of my grandfather's courthouse standing above the trees.

"That's not it, George," I shouted down to the navigator, "that's Mercer, if you can find it on the map."

He studied the map. "Turn left!" he yelled over the roar of the engines. I banked the plane to the east, away from Mercer.

Judd yelled, "Turn west! Turn west! Where in the heck are you going?"

"I thought you said 'Turn *left!*'"

"Don't you know where the heck your own hometown is?" Oats laughed.

Now we were really feeling lost. I swung back.

Gradually I began to recognize the lay of the land. There was Mercer, on our right now. There was the road going out of town to the southwest. That should put New Wilmington just about over there ... beyond those hills over there. I headed straight for them. Yes, that should be it. I came down lower still. Yes! There was New Wilmington spread out in the valley before us.

A Pathway through the Sky

I flew straight for the ridge where my home stands. We thundered down over the hill and headed straight over the heart of town. People started racing out of their houses to find out what in the world was going on. Below us now was the park in the center of town ... and the tower on Westminster College campus. We roared right on out the other side of the valley and up over the hills.

I turned steeply 180 degrees and headed back in. This time we would make the drop. I alerted Bill Flesey in the waist position. Down we went, down very low indeed, only a few feet over the houses and trees. I flew straight for the park in the center of town.

"Now!" I yelled to Flesey. With a terrific heave, he sent the pillow case tumbling out of the camera hatch into the air. He just caught sight of it as it landed right on the grass. We had hit our first target perfectly ...

We were up again and over the hill. I turned back for one last pass. There was our home, old "Stone Gables". *Wait a minute! There was Mom! There was Mom! ... and Bill too!* ... There they were, on the lawn. Mom was waving her apron. I shifted the pitch of the four propellers back and forth. The engines responded with an almighty roar which must have been heard all down the valleys. I waggled the wings in farewell and pulled up and away.

We left New Wilmington and rose over the hills. It was still a perfect morning.

... Far below, I could make out old Chautauqua Lake. I wondered if the old rowboat we used to own was still tied up there. We flew on towards Westover, climbing up steadily into the blue summer sky.

Quietly I said goodbye – goodbye to home and to 19 years of memories that went with it. ... We were on our way to the war

Down below us now were the fields of Scotland. The sun slanted in long shafts through the cotton clouds, creating striking patterns of light and shadow on the green earth below. Farms and houses, fields and fences, forest and fen, all slipped beneath our wing, etched in exquisite detail in the warm yellow lakes of afternoon sunshine. It was breath-taking.

We dropped down and came in for our landing.

Once on the ground, we quickly disembarked and turned over our equipment and the plane we had flown across the Atlantic to the authorities at the base. The clouds were rolling in fast, and as we drove down the country roads to the railway station, the first drops of rain began to fall.

We boarded the train with our duffle-bags and cases. Due to the danger of air raids, our carriage was blacked out and we raced on and on through that night, not knowing where we were headed or where we were.

Early the next morning our train pulled into a staging depot where we were held for several days before being sent on to Belfast, Ireland, for further training.

Ireland was lovely in those mid-summer days. Our barracks were spilled across the countryside on the low hills near Belfast. Here, during the next weeks, we went through ground training in different radio and navigational devices and aids that were in current use in Great Britain during that stage of the war. We had long hours of spare time, giving us chances to talk and read, and to get to know each other better.

Finally the day came when we were flown across the Irish Sea to England. We were assigned to the 392nd Bombardment Group, based at a former Royal Air Force base at Wendling in the heart of rural Norfolk in East Anglia.

We landed at our base and taxied over to a vacant hardstand. The engines ticked over to a standstill and immediately we scrambled out, tumbling to the ground from the hatch. Somehow, it felt like the first day at school.

There were the bombers – old B-24s lined up around the edge of the field. We walked over to them, studying them with awe and wonder. They looked like old war veterans, tired and weary, staring down at us with bloodshot hollow eyes. Here and there we noticed scars on the wing surfaces and fuselages … bullet-holes, shrapnel from flak bursts. As we walked past, our footsteps seemed to echo with the footsteps of men who had gone before, with memories of planes that were here no more and of crews that had vanished in the mud of France.

The field had two runways. They crossed by a stand of ageless sinewy oaks, tall and brooding. The perimeter track wound its way around the edge of the field, connecting the four ends of the runways. Rising over the low roof of the headquarters building was the old gray control tower, standing watch over all.

The field was typical of most American bases in Great Britain. It had been an RAF training base before the war. The officer's club and dining hall and the infirmary were permanent structures, built with concrete and stone. Spread out over the rest of the two-square-mile base area were the temporary buildings, the 20-by-70 foot corrugated tin huts in which we, the bomber crews, lived. The area for the enlisted men, the ground personnel area, and the area for flying officers were separated by various strips of cultivated farming land.

Ours was a funny-looking little prefabricated building, built of gabled tin, its curved roof drooping down sadly to the ground, a few cheerless windows looking out. We went inside. There were four compartments. Oats and I were to occupy one, and Judd and Hank Streicher the connecting compartments.

We quickly got the little coal stove going as the evening air, rolling in from the sea, was chill and bitter.

We settled in and then biked down to supper. After supper, our commanding officer, Colonel Lorin Johnson, came around for a brief word. Tomorrow, he said, we would have a practice flight. We would have a chance to get acclimatized to our surrounding area, to become familiar with the land around our field. It would also be our first chance to rehearse combat formation flying.

The weather in East Anglia, he told us, was apt to change suddenly. Often great fog banks would roll in from the sea at a moment's notice. We would learn how to use the navigational aids for landing in use at our base.

"Get a good night's sleep," he said. There was scattered applause and we got up and shuffled out of the hall.

The next morning, we had our first chance to see a mission take off from our own field. At five o'clock the lead plane thundered down the strip, its bomb bay filled with a full bomb-load, its tanks chock-full with 2,600 gallons of gas. I held my breath as it lifted into the air at the very end of the runway, clearing the fence and the surrounding trees by a small margin.

One by one the planes moved out at 30-second intervals. We watched them climbing up into the air with a droning thunder, hundreds of aircraft, reaching up to 12,000 feet above us in the sky.

Finally, the bomber group turned east, heading in the direction of the continent.

... Our first mission came a few days later.

Standing left to right: Sgt. Robert J. Flesey, waist gunner; Sgt. Robert P. O'Kane, waist gunner; S/Sgt. James F. Fender, radio operator; S/Sgt. William D. Drummond, engineer; S/Sgt. Charles McNeill, gunner; Sgt. Sylvester Luciano; tail gunner. Kneeling, left to right: 2Lt. Henry P. Streicher Jr., bombardier/navigator; 2Lt. James A. McLaughry, copilot; 2Lt. Otho L. summers, pilot; 2Lt George G. Judd, navigator.

Chapter 3

Our First Mission

"Breakfast at three, briefing at four, sir."

The staff sergeant was shaking me awake. A cold draft of air was flooding in the open door of our Nissen hut.

"Yes, okay, okay," I grumbled. The sergeant slammed the door as he walked out.

I rolled over to look at the clock. 2:30 a.m. Up through the small window, I could see the sky, pitch black, moonless and still, a thin fleece of cirrus covering the stars. We were going on a mission today ... into the heart of Germany. Eight or nine hours in the air. We would be back before dusk, if we were lucky.

... Could it only have been three or four hours ago that we turned off the lights and went to sleep?

I struggled to the edge of my bed and pulled on my clothes. They were damp and soggy from the East Anglia atmosphere. Oats and I got on our bikes outside and headed down the macadam road in the darkness. The mess hall was three-quarters of a mile away.

Eggs for breakfast. Fresh eggs. Every morning before a combat mission we would get fresh eggs. The other days there would be dried powdered eggs.

We ate the warm food with relish.

Outside after breakfast, the sky was still dark with only the faintest hint of dawn in the east. It was another long half mile down the road to the base headquarters over the blacked out countryside.

We parked our bikes and walked into the locker room, our flying boots clattering on the wooden floor-boards. The cold glare of the electric light bulbs bruised my eyes with the sudden brilliance. I went over to my locker and pulled down my electrically-heated flying clothes, my flak jacket and gloves, the oxygen mask and the helmet hanging on the wall.

... It was SO early in the morning. Every fourth breath seemed to be a yawn.

In the briefing hall, there was a low drone of conversation, interrupted by the occasional outbursts of laughter here and there. All the different crews in our group were assembling, 450 men.

I sat down at my table. The officer in charge rapped for silence and the briefing began.

"Today," he said, "our target will be an aircraft engine plant." He drew back the curtain covering the large map of the European continent on the wall. A long red ribbon stretched from our base, out over the North Sea, into the heart of industrial Germany. Stuttgart! That was a long way in ... I heard the groans of a few individuals behind me. Our Initial Point was shown on the map. The exact location of our target was described to us, as well as the course we were to take over the continent.

The weather officer was called up. There would be a cloud layer at about 14,000 feet over the continent, he told us. We could expect tail winds at 21,000 feet, our flying altitude. On our way back during the afternoon, we would meet the same headwind, but, "On the whole," he said, "you can expect fine weather all day."

There was considerable chatter at the back of the hall. "Remember what happened the last time fair weather was forecast?" "Remember that 'cloud cover' at 15,000 feet last time? Worst storm we ever came through." "...'Clear weather'? Haven't we've heard that before?"

Next came the flak briefing. We could expect heavy concentrations of enemy anti-aircraft artillery over the Rhine River as usual. Fighter attacks would be most likely in about a fifty-mile radius of the Nuremburg area. Opposition, however, was unlikely to be very heavy today due to the fact that ...

Again there was a disturbance at the back of the hall. What good were flak briefings anyway? Things never turned out the way they were predicted!

The officer in charge rapped his wooden pointer on the desk.

Last of all, we were briefed on the codes, the radio frequencies and the signal flares we were to use. We were to keep strictest radio silence on the way in and the way out. We were to use blue and yellow flares today to indicate wounded aboard. Our group identification flares would be red and yellow. We were given the frequency of the VHF fighter-bomber radio channel. Blue and green flares were to be used in case of emergency need for fighter assistance.

We were dismissed. I walked on over to the desk and turned in my wallet and Air Force ring for safe-keeping during the day.

I looked around the room. Loud laughter was ringing to the rafters from many groups. Some of those guys would not come back tonight I guessed ... Would it be the other guys' crew? Or would it be our own? That's what was really on my mind.

Laughter didn't completely succeed in covering up what others were feeling. I knew we were all going through the same turmoil.

Outside on the field, the giant gasoline trucks were pulling back into the pens. Refueling operations had gone on all night and during the small hours of the morning. I heard the quiet hum of engines and the occasional snarl of a jeep as it raced across the perimeter track from one plane to another in the early morning light. The air was fresh and moist. I took a deep breath.

We swung aboard the crowded base truck that was to take us to the plane we had been assigned to, and rumbled out across the field.

"Thar' she blows!" Punch yelled. "Gashouse Gus! Waaaa hoo!"

A Pathway through the Sky

We bailed out. There she was, our plane, with 17 missions painted in black beside the cockpit window, one bomb to represent each mission. The ground crew absolutely adored the ship. They had spared nothing in displaying their art in fantastic pictures on the fuselage.

Our crew scrambled into the plane and began the thorough overall examination of every detail. There was a check list which we had to go through twice. Everything had to be tested, the oxygen tanks and pressures, the individual electrical outlets, the gun casings, the hydraulic system, and a hundred other items.

The sky was washed with grey light now. It was five o'clock. Oats and I sat chatting on the cement hardstand underneath the wing. The rest of the crew were in the plane or sitting on the grass near the hardstand.

Only minutes before zero hour a truck drew up beside the plane. Judd and Streicher had been at a special briefing for navigators and bombardiers. Hank arrived, completely out of breath, carrying three flak suits under his arm. A roar of laughter went up from the crew.

"What's the big idea of all the flak suits?" Punchy yelled.

Hank winked as he clambered into the hatch. "You guys can laugh, but I'm not taking any chances!"

We all climbed in.

Zero hour came and we took off into the gray of the morning. Our squadron assembled high over the field and by 0754 hours we were headed out over the North Sea, on our way to the continent.

Time passed slowly. We were going deep into Germany today. Against the ever-increasing light of morning, I could see hundreds of aircraft on every side, beneath us and behind. Our formation was moving over the Initial Point. We altered course a few degrees and settled into level steady flight, heading straight for our target.

The bombardier was making final adjustments before advancing over the bomb run. We closed into formation a little more tightly.

Then, we were over the bomb run. I eased the throttles forward. Steady now. Keep your eyes off that flak and on the next plane ahead of you. Okay. *Now!* The bombs hurtled down through the open doors of the hatch and dropped down, down, through the sky. *Close her up! Close her up!* We need every bit of speed we can get.

The flak was floating inquiringly up. Our formation thundered around in a 120 degree turn and headed back for England. *Thank God there were no fighters up here today!*

Suddenly there was a tremendous WHOOMP! on the plane. It was a complete surprise – no black smoke or flak puffs nearby.

Bill Flesey cried out over the intercom, "Waist gunner to pilot – *I'm hit!*"

Instants later, a second message came. "Navigator to pilot – *I'm hit!*" It was George Judd down in the nose.

A wave of coldness flooded over me.

"Pilot to engineer. Pilot to engineer. Go down and see what you can do for the waist gunner." Oats tersely snapped out the orders. "Pilot to bombardier, look after the navigator."

Quickly Bill Drummond jumped down from the top turret position and put on his walk-around oxygen bottle. Hank Streicher climbed down from the nose turret to look after Judd.

We flew on, panic at our hearts' door.

I looked around. None of the engines had been hit. Mechanically everything was still in order.

"Hurry the hell up back there!"

Drummond was working his way back through the bomb bays. He got back to the waist position and found the two waist gunners. Flesey had been badly hit. A piece of shrapnel had torn deep into his right side, tearing off a large piece of flesh from his right arm. He was in considerable pain.

Nearby, O'Kane, the other waist gunner, was lying unconscious. His oxygen supply line had been hit and broken.

Drummond worked fast. He quickly gave Bill Flesey a shot of morphine and ran an extension of the other oxygen supply down to O'Kane.

This was our first experience of flak as a crew. We weren't ready for it. We were numbed and shocked.

Streicher was working on the navigator. He succeeded in locating a small wound on his left leg and quickly dressed it. Judd refused to take morphine and insisted on navigating the return flight.

We stuck closely in formation. Each minute was agony for Bill in the waist. Judd was in terrible pain.

It was cruel how slowly the hours passed.

About three quarters of the way back to England, O'Kane began to revive. He had been a professional boxer before the war and was reliving it again. He was in the ring and swinging hard at anything in sight. There was a big scuffle back in the waist. Drummond eventually calmed him down.

Once over our field, we fired the Very pistol to indicate wounded aboard. We were quickly given clearance and landed. As we pulled into our hardstand, I could see the ambulance racing across the field.

The flight surgeon came on board and immediately went back to the waist position. Bill Flesey was stretched out in serious condition. Shrapnel from the flak burst had torn through his body only inches away from his heart. It had been very close.

Bill was lowered down from the plane and carried by stretcher bearers to the ambulance.

George Judd was in very severe pain. His pant leg was soaked

Our First Mission

with blood. The surgeon quickly cut the pant leg off and discovered a deep angry wound in his thigh of which he had been unaware. Judd was quickly given morphine and eased down out of the hatch to the ground.

I jumped down and watched the ambulance move off with Bill and George inside.

This had been our first experience of enemy action in combat.

I found my stomach as hard as rock ....

Chapter 4

Skies of Fire and Death

Bill Flesey, our waist gunner, was in the infirmary for over a month convalescing from his wounds of the previous mission. Our navigator, George Judd, whom we prided as one of the best navigators in our squadron, was in the infirmary for three weeks after the same mission. For that period, Henry Streicher, our bombardier, was the navigator of our crew.

During the succeeding missions, we began to experience the Germans' shrewdness and cunning in air tactics.

We were en route to our target area one day - our fourth mission. We had made our change of course at the Initial Point, and were in straight and level flight, flying on the left wing of the lead plane.

Punchy called up on the intercom. "Waist gunner to pilot, waist gunner to pilot. Straggler at seven o'clock high."

I looked out of my window. Sure enough, trailing behind the squadron was another B-24, lagging behind as if in mechanical difficulty of some nature. It looked strange.

We moved in toward the target.

Suddenly, the straggler turned steeply to the left and dived down very quickly. We just caught sight of him as he screamed down to the deck.

Oats swore. "That was a damn Jerry flying that plane."

It must have been. Instants later, we flew right into a colossal barrage of flak. The sky turned black with exploding steel and smoke on every side. All hell was bursting loose. Every last anti aircraft gun in the area was letting go, right smack into the heart of our formation.

Our squadron leader veered to his right - there was a big cloud of flak dead ahead.

"Oh, you crazy fool!" Oats shouted.

No sooner had he turned than another huge eruption of flak bursts appeared dead ahead of him. In the madness of the moment, I was tempted to turn off from his wing to avoid the fragments hurtling through the air. But we flew on through.

Suddenly, we were out the other side. I looked around. Miraculously, our squadron had come through unscathed. We were over the target and dropped our bombs.

The German crew in the reconditioned B-24 "straggler" had been able to radio our exact position, altitude and speed to the anti-aircraft batteries on the ground. The flak had been terribly accurate. Several planes in our wing went down that day.

It was a clever trick - one we were careful to avoid in the future.

Back on base in the debriefing room, we would have to tell the whole terrible story. We had seen one of our planes disappear into a cloud of flak. What came out the other side was nothing but a confusion of blazing, falling steel. There couldn't have been any survi-baysvors.

... Another plane was hit in the Number Three engine and the propeller was quickly feathered. We managed to keep sight of the damaged plane until we got out over the North Sea. It was apparent the pilot was having trouble with his Number One engine. Suddenly the plane caught on fire and rolled over on its back and went down.

... The poor guys didn't have time to bail out.

After such missions, we would walk from the debriefing room outside to the bicycle rack. We would see many bikes standing unused. The men - the boys, really – who had ridden them down early that morning would not be back.

A few mornings later, we were taking off for a strike over Germany. As we thundered down the runway in the gray dawn, I noticed that our Number One engine was not pulling maximum power. Quickly, we cut all four throttles back and brought the plane to a halt, pulling off the runway to make room for the rest of the planes that were following at regular intervals.

We taxied over to the hardstand. Our ground crew went to work fast and picked out the trouble. It would take a long time to fix. We called in for instructions and were immediately assigned another plane.

As we swung aboard the second bomber, it was easy to see that it had been through a number of missions and was old, scarred and battered.

We took off, climbed up to altitude and moved in with our formation. The bomber wing moved out over the English coast. As we climbed steadily to higher altitudes over the continent, I noticed our engines were beginning to act up. At about 14,000 feet, we began to lag behind the rest of the formation.

I called up the engineer. "Can't you give us any more power, Bill?" We were drifting about 75 yards behind the plane ahead of us.

"It's those superchargers, Mac. If you ask me, we never should have taken this old crate up in the first place."

Instead of having electronic superchargers as on new B-24s, this older aircraft had oil-operated manual superchargers. They were not functioning properly. The oil was gradually thickening and stiffening due to the cold, and as a result, the superchargers failed to produce the necessary compression for the engines.

We turned in over the bomb run. Luckily, there was no serious antiaircraft action from below that day. The flak batteries around the target seemed fairly inactive. We dropped our load and banked around with the formation back towards home.

We were not far from the target area when our engines worsened considerably. Our efficiency fell way down. It became impossible to keep up with our formation. We would have to go down. It was the only thing left to do.

We peeled off from our squadron and descended. Down below, a dull undercast covered the earth. The clouds were unbroken to the horizon.

After some time, I called to Streicher in the nose. "Co-pilot to bombardier. Co-pilot to bombardier. Can you give us an approximate location?"

Streicher was poring over the maps and navigation instruments, desperately trying to give us some idea of where to go. His voice was plaintive with dismay, "I don't know *where* we are!"

Our altitude was now 10,000 feet and we were still losing height. Our engines would not hold out much longer. We needed to get behind our own lines as quickly as we could, find some field and land. ... Meanwhile, we were going down into Germany, all alone.

Oats and I decided that, despite the dangers involved, we should try to draw our own fighters to us for assistance. The trouble was, emergency flares were just as likely to bring enemy fighters as our own. But we had to risk that.

The Very pistol was fired and two brilliant globes of colored gas fell through the air. Any enemy fighter for miles around could have seen them.

... We waited.

"Tail gunner to pilot. Two aircraft sighted at approximately 23,000 feet."

"Where?"

"Coming in now from 5 o'clock high." ... I held my breath.

"Yes, I see them." It was O'Kane in the waist. "P-51's aren't they?"

They had better be, I thought. We were utterly unprotected against enemy attack from the air. ... I could see them now. They *were* P-51's - probably from some weather reconnaissance group.

"What a beautiful sight!" Streicher was jubilant.

We watched them coming in. It was a terrific relief to have the "little brothers" alongside. They flew in on our left wing and came level with us.

We quickly made contact over the VHF bomber-to-fighter channel. Oats described our predicament. Our superchargers were acting up. We had to land fast. Could they give us any idea of where we were and how to get to some field nearby behind the lines?

The reply came back in a Texas drawl. They were sorry, but they didn't know where *they* were either! Maybe the best thing would be to go ahead, find a hole in the cloud cover, go down and find out.

We agreed with the plan. The Texan waggled his wings and pulled off. We watched the pair of fighters diving down into the thick white cotton clouds. We lost sight of them and flew on for about ten minutes. ... Soon they were back.

Yes, he had located himself, the Texan said. He would take us in. There was a field behind our lines, not too far away.

We followed him down through the cloud cover. A heavy thunderstorm was blackening the countryside. Rain was drenching down in sheets and the wind was driving in violent gusts across the earth. We lumbered on through the weather, only 1,500 feet above the fields. Our engines were steadily growing worse. We flew and flew and flew for what seemed an eternity of time.

I called in to the lead pilot of the P-51's. "Are we getting there?"

"We'll be there any minute now."

"Are you sure you know where you are?"

He was flying on our left. I saw him turn in the cockpit and look at us. "Well, I think so."

Think so? "Well, I hope to *hell* you know where you are!"

This couldn't go on much longer. The engines were just about ready to blank out altogether – all four of them. I put on my crash harness. We might have to choose some poor farmer's field as a landing strip. It could happen very suddenly.

Ten miles behind the front lines in Belgium, there was an airfield. It was used as a supply point for front line troops. Ammunition and weapons were being flown in ceaselessly night and day. The lead pilot of the P-51's was taking us to this field in the hopes we could land.

We got in radio range of the control tower. It was impossible to get through. The Germans had jammed the frequency with raucous American jazz. Overhead, I could see the sky filled with C-47's coming in with full loads, impatiently trying to get to the ground. It was no use. Chances seemed slim we could break through to get permission to land. We didn't have much power to make a second pass.

Then the lead pilot of the P-51's radioed to us, "Stick around, Mac! We'll get you down!" Immediately, the two fighter pilots headed straight for a cloud of incoming C-47's. They screamed right smack into the traffic pattern.

"That's right! That's right!" Streicher was shouting. "Scare hell out of 'em!"

The transport planes veered helter-skelter off in all directions, scattering out across the fields. Suddenly, the airspace was clear and there was room to land. We let down the flaps and dropped down onto the end of the runway, directly behind another C-47. The spray from his wheels sheeted our windshield with muddy water. We turned off immediately onto the grass to avoid hitting him from behind, and rolled a long way over the field.

I was on the radio, sending thanks to the fighter pilots. "Well, we finally made it to the continent of Europe, boys, thanks to you. Great to be here. Anything we can do for you, now we're on the ground?"

There was instant enthusiasm from the fighter pilots. "Sure is!" came the reply. "How about some 'Chanel Number Five' if you can get some?"

"Some *what*?"

"'Chanel Number Five', Mac. They probably sell it down there somewhere."

It was a bit ridiculous. I watched the P-51's streaking up out of sight beyond the field. "Sure, okay. Where do we send it?"

He gave me his code number and base. "They all know me, Mac."

"Wilco!" I turned the radio off.

A truck came over to pick us up after we had parked the plane. As we bounced across the rain-soaked airfield, I saw tens of parked B-24's and B-17's, lined up in mournful rows. Many planes had force-landed into Belgium, just as we had. There was quite a supply of them.

The truck headed out from the field and down a rutted, muddy road to the army mess hall. It was my first time in Europe. I stared with curiosity at the scenery and the people we saw. There was a gray look of war on everything ... on people's faces as well as in the features of the landscape. The fighting had left its mark of horror in men's eyes as well as on their ruined homes and farms. My! It tore my heart to see the peasant children staring at us as we sped down that road – starved and weary, wanting to hope, but not daring to trust.

We had lunch at the mess. As we got up to leave, two men came in wearing fighter pilot uniforms. Oats nudged me. "Those must be the guys who brought us in."

Henry Streicher couldn't contain himself and walked straight up to them. "Say, are you the guys who flew us in? The P-51's?"

They nodded and smiled. Streicher immediately threw his arms around the senior officer and hugged him again and again. When he wrenched himself free, the officer and the pilot flying his wing came over to meet us. Apparently they had run low on gas and had been forced to land at this field to get fuel. They had come in for some hot food before continuing. We were introduced all around and stood chatting for a few minutes.

"Give my regards to Colonel Johnson," the senior pilot said as we headed out the door. (Colonel Lorin L. Johnson was our commanding officer ... we didn't see much of him.)

"Fine," I replied. "Who shall we say is sending his regards?"

"I am Colonel ___, Commanding Officer of the ___ Weather Reconnaissance Group," he said. "Johnson knows me."

Streicher quickly ducked out the door. A colonel? How was he to know that when he hugged him? As we drove back to the airfield in the truck, I saw Streicher staring out the back. Strange how quiet he had become, I thought ...

We climbed on board a B-24 that we had been assigned to fly back to England. The fuselage was shredded with bullet-holes. There were no cushions on the pilots' seats, just the bare armor plating. I noticed several blood marks. Someone had really had a bad time of it.

We took off into the rain and climbed up to altitude. It was a three hour flight through turbulent weather and thundershowers back to England. ... We arrived on our own base late that afternoon.

Chapter 5

The Voice of God in Combat

The next day was our day off. Overhead the sky was bleak and dull. Large white rain-drops were pelting down out of the sky, pattering coldly on the tin roof. Water skidded down the window-panes in jagged rivulets. The mud was deep on the roads, and the first autumn leaves were hurrying from drenched trees in the wind.

"We were right over the bomb run. Flak wasn't too bad – just a little smudge here and there. We got the word, and opened her up to drop our payload."

The speaker was a first pilot in our squadron. Just yesterday he had come in from a mission over Germany. His plane had been hit and had gone down in flames. He was telling me the whole story.

"I remember the bombardier yelling, 'Bombs away!'", he said. "Instants later - WHAM! The whole plane lurched wildly out of control. She flipped into a dive. I hauled up on the stick and hung on for dear life. The ship had kinda' lifted up behind and was pitched over. My co-pilot grabbed the other wheel and we just clutched on as hard as we could, struggling to keep the nose up."

"What had happened?"

"Well, Mac, it was a freak accident. We were in a very tight formation. There was another Liberator right above us. When he let go of his bombs, they came crashing down on our tail section and knocked half of it clean off. My waist gunner called up and said the whole left side of the elevator and stabilizer was gone."

"How in the world did you keep flying?" I asked.

"I don't know. I'll never know. But she did. We gave her a little more power on one side and hung on to that stick all the way back. My arms were just about breaking off. I didn't think I'd ever be able to move my wrists or hands again. They're still as stiff as hell."

He looked down at his hands and tried to work his fingers.

"It was agonizing. Many times we didn't think we could hold on any longer. But of course we had to. We *had* to.

"Then we reached England." He got up and walked over to the window and looked out, clearing the steam from the glass with his gloves. "I still don't know how we pulled through."

He stared out at the countryside, drawing a deep breath. "I guess, Mac, I had one in a thousand chances. All I know is that I was praying like I never had before."

As he spoke, I was remembering our experience on August 24th when we had literally come in on a wing and a prayer.

He turned around. "Our base was weathered in, as you know. The ceiling was right down a few feet off the deck and it was squally as hell. We were careening through the fog, trying to make our way.

"We got in touch with the tower. They told us to try another field nearby. When we got there, the weather was just as bad; the visibility was right down to zero. We were getting low on gas. I turned in and started coming in on a regular instrument let-down."

He walked over to the stove. "Mac, you try bringing in a four-engine bomber in a fog like that with half your tail-section gone!"

"We came on in – down, down. Suddenly, right next to us in the fog, I saw a huge black water tower. It scared the daylights out of me. Visibility was so low that I hadn't seen it until we were right on it – only feet away. I yanked her over, hard to the left. I guess we didn't miss it by more than a wingspan.

"That was too much for me. I gave up the idea of trying to bring that old wreck in for a landing. I'd probably just make a flaming mess on somebody's runway. I wasn't going to go on fooling around in that fog in a crippled 'Lib, especially with nine men aboard.

"So we headed up and got the hell out of there.

"When we got up to about 7,000 feet, I gave the order for the crew to bail out. They moved to the open bomb bay door. It was the first jump for all of those guys. One by one, they dropped free and their parachutes opened up behind us.

"Now, just the co-pilot and I were left. I told him to hang on to that stick with all his might. I got out of my seat and came around behind it. Then, leaning forward, I grabbed onto the stick tightly and told him to scramble – to bail out as quickly as he could. He moved back to the bomb bay and flung himself down into space.

"I was alone, all alone in that broken up old bomber, flying through the sky with her on her last trip. I let go of the wheel, and in the same instant, I tried to dive for the door. But the plane nosed over into a spin. I was pinned. I couldn't move. I was pressed against the top bulkhead. All four engines were screaming like all the devils in hell and the old bomber was pulling full power straight for the ground.

"Then a fire broke out in the bomb-bay."

He was silent for a moment, staring at the coal stove.

"Mac, there was absolutely nothing I could do. The plane was screaming down to the ground. The fire was getting closer. I couldn't budge an inch, though God knows I was trying with all my strength.

"I started praying and I told God, 'Look, if You want me to get out of this, You've got to do something quick. There isn't anything that I can do.'

He looked at me. "Maybe that wasn't much of a prayer. But, at that very instant, the left wing split off. The plane turned crazily over on its side, and in those few seconds, I was able to crawl back through the blazing fire and drop out through the bomb-bay.

"I fell and fell. Flaming fragments and falling steel whistled down through the air. I pulled my rip-cord. My 'chute opened just a little ways above the trees and I tumbled down through the branches to solid ground.

"Instants earlier, the bomber had slammed into a nearby field and was completely destroyed."

The experiences I and others had had in combat convinced me that there was a God and that He could speak over the roar of the engines and guide us and take away our fear.

We had come through so many close calls in combat. Fourteen times out of twenty-one missions, we had come back with wounded aboard, or flying on fewer than four engines, or crippled with mechanical difficulty due to enemy action.

... I had believed in God all my life. But I had never really had a deeply personal experience of His power and grace.

Then, on August 24th, 1944, flying in combat, we faced death as a crew. In a desperate moment, I asked God for His direction and guidance. He spoke clearly to me, telling me what to do. He took away my fear. I was convinced the Hand of God was guiding us as we came home.

I thought back to that restless, sleepless night of August 24th after we landed.

The luminous radium dial of the old alarm clock glowed dully beside my bed. It was well past midnight.

I turned over again for what must have been the thirtieth time. For some reason, I had been unable to get any sleep. The extreme tensions and anxieties of the day had left me taut and restless and, though I tried, I had utterly failed to relax.

All sorts of thoughts tumbled and twisted and rambled through my head as I lay there ... that awful moment when our Number One engine was hit and burst into flames ... the crazy convulsions of the aircraft immediately afterwards ... the evil black clouds of smoke frothing from the nacelle. I sweated when I thought of it. It was touch and go whether the flames would reach our gas tanks and destroy us all in one horrible, blinding, scalding instant.

Then, there was the worse torture of the long flight back when there was nothing but the constant pulsating roar of the engines, and the huge empty room of the sky – a terrible sky in which lurked hidden dangers, the lead-spitting fighters diving unexpectedly from the sun, the purple-black puffs of flak bouncing up in a terrifyingly accurate cobweb on every side.

I thought of the 121st Psalm. In many moments of extreme danger, it had come to mean very much to me – especially the last verse: "The Lord shall preserve thy going out and thy coming in from this time forth and even forevermore."

I began to think of the amazing experience of God's voice speaking aloud to me. I had been in desperate need. I was filled with terrible fear. I did not know what to do. I was at the end of my own courage and strength. More than anything else, I needed God's help and direction. What was I to do with the engines? How was I to handle the plane? What was I to tell the men?

My need had been met and answered in every last detail. Think of it! We had been headed for a seemingly inevitable open-sea ditching. Miraculously, we had avoided a mid-air collision. We had been swung off our predestined course just *exactly* enough to head our plane straight for our own base. We had landed with one and a half minutes of flying time to spare.

It had truly been a "miracle mission".

Yes ... but there would be more missions. There would be more flak, more fighters. Could we depend on this Source for strength every time? Was God present in every situation?

The Voice of God in Combat

I rolled over. A blast of cold damp East Anglia air crawled down my neck and invaded the warmth of my blankets.

Slowly, I began to see before my eyes falling snow-flakes – a confusion of snowflakes, tumbling down in twisting dizzying clouds to the street. It was mid-January 1942 again. It was past two o'clock in the morning and I was standing underneath an old street lamp talking to a friend of mine. We had been talking for a long time …

"The question is, Jimmy," he was saying, "whether you are willing to give God control of every part of your life – from tonight on – forever."

I knew my friend had made that decision. He was a radiant man, a man of profound joy and liberty. In my heart, I deeply wanted to be like him, to live the triumphant life of obedience that he was living.

And yet …

I gazed at an old fire hydrant under a huge heavy blanket of snow just outside the ring of light from the street lamp. "Yes, you're right," I said. "I know you're right. I know I should let God guide my life. I know this is what the nation needs." I looked into his face. "But," I said, "I am enjoying the way I am living and I don't want God or anyone else to interfere."

At that moment, I somehow turned my back on God. My heart had felt as cold and solid as that frozen old fire hydrant in the snow.

I rolled over again. It was hard to keep warm. In the distance, I heard the drone of an aircraft flying low over the sleeping countryside … I thought of the reconnaissance patrols starting out at dawn tomorrow. They would retrace our trail into the heart of Germany. Their photographs might prove beyond any doubt that we had missed the target, that the factories we had meant to hit were still erect and undamaged. It would mean that a whole day's effort of materiel and man-power had been of no avail. We would have to do the same thing all over again another day to make up for the mistakes.

It had happened before.

Perhaps, too, I was going to look back on my life at the age of eighty, only to find that *I* had missed the target - that my energies had been wasted and my true destiny lost forever. Perhaps that would be the story of my generation in this world.

Chapter 6

A New Mission in Life

Not many nights later, after another harrowing day of combat, I again lay awake longer than usual. Despite my extraordinary experience of God speaking to me in combat and leading us home safely, I was not yet convinced that I wanted to give my entire life to Him. It was as though I were standing at the edge of a high dive over a swimming pool - my fears whispered in my ears, and I did not dare to make the plunge.

Eventually I grew quiet and began to listen. Fresh thoughts came into my head. They were as clear and concise as though they had been spoken to me by someone in the room.

"Are you willing, Jim, to go back into combat and to be killed if that is God's will?'

"Are you ready to go to the Pacific and fly another tour of missions?" (It happened to be the thing I most dreaded.)

"Are you willing to be a ditch-digger for the rest of your life if God asks it?"

At the last thought, I chuckled. I would rather be *anything* but a ditch-digger. In high school, I had been the president of my senior class, editor of the school newspaper, leader of a church group. In college, I had pushed my way to positions of leadership. After the war was over, my big ambition was to enter politics and climb the ladder to success.

For several moments, I still could not make up my mind. I still balked at the top of the diving board, unwilling to jump. Yet I realized that my whole future depended on whether I refused or accepted what God was asking me.

... Then, quietly I whispered the words, "I will." I thought of the three questions that had come to my mind. I answered them one by one. "Yes, I am ready to be killed in combat. I am ready to go to the Pacific. I am ready to be a ditch-digger for the rest of my life. I am ready to do anything that God wills."

I finally leapt from that imaginary diving board. Instantly, peace and calmness flooded over me. I felt released in my heart, a new man. I had never felt quite so happy in my life.

Soon, I was fast asleep, resting as peacefully as a child.

I woke the next day, greatly refreshed ... and still thinking. In the early morning quietness, I decided to take the next step in my life. I made up my mind to get in touch with the international team of Moral Re-Armament at their London headquarters.

On a three day leave not long after, I went to London and phoned the MRA center. I was invited for supper. I jumped in a small cab and made my way through the teeming city to Berkeley Square. It was a beautiful park, small and quiet, right in the heart of the West End. 45 Berkeley Square was a lovely old home facing the park.

I was met at the door and welcomed in.

There I met people who were passionately concerned with the state of the world; people who had laid down their lives and given their possessions to bring an answer; people who lived the quality of life they longed to see in the world. They were exuberant, warm-hearted and welcoming people. They had a clear purpose in life.

I found myself discussing many things with them: What was the whole purpose of our being in Europe at that time? What was the purpose of the war? What would the end of the fighting bring? Would it really bring peace?

A New Mission in Life

Most of my friends and I were about twenty years old. In our missions over Germany and occupied Europe I had seen many planes go down. I had seen whole crews die in combat. I couldn't get the horrifying images out of my mind.

Would there really be peace in the world when we had done away with Hitler? Or with Mussolini? They were just two men who were able to concentrate a fanatic, driving, ruthless power over millions of people and mobilize a terrible, brutal military machine for their evil purposes.

America was out to gain a victory in arms. But after this war was over, would America return to a comfortable way of life, unchanged by this unimaginably horrible world-wide catastrophe? Would my children be forced to fight in an even more terrible war than I had – a Third World War – simply because we, as a nation, did not dare to change?

William Penn once said, "Men will either choose to be governed by God, or they condemn themselves to be ruled by tyrants."

What would America answer?

While I was at the Berkeley Square headquarters, I tried listening to God with another man. We sat quietly with pencil and paper, ready to note down all the thoughts that came in to our minds. At first I felt foolish. But deep in my heart, I knew I was doing the most sensible thing that any human being can do ... to listen to the voice of the Lord for direction.

One thought came. I wrote it down and looked at it. *"Roger."*

My English friend asked what the word meant.

"It means 'yes'," I said. "It means 'Yes, I will. I will comply'. It means God's will and no longer my own."

A Pathway through the Sky

The first step was dramatic. I began to rise earlier every morning back on base to listen to His voice. I listened for an hour. I wrote down on a piece of paper every last thought that came to mind. I determined to heed the thoughts that I wrote down, and to act on them before the day was out.

One morning not long after, we were at our stations in the ship. Zero hour was approaching and we were busy checking through the last minute details. In a few moments, we would be taking off for another mission deep into Germany.

As I was sitting in the cockpit, a thought came to me, "Drill the waist gunner!"

We had been supplied with a spare waist gunner that day, a replacement for Bill Flesey who was still in the infirmary. I did not know him. It was true that he hadn't struck me as being a man of much courage or technical competence. But it would be a foolish thing to drill him. What would he think? What would the crew think?

Of course, when an engine was hit in combat, a waist gunner would be more likely to see it before either Oats or I would. Both engines on his side would be in full view. We would need to act immediately if an engine was hit and a fire broke out. Our lives could depend on having an adequate report from our spare waist gunner.

I decided to obey the thought, and made my way to the waist position. I stood with the waist gunner looking out at the engines.

"Which is engine Number One?" I asked.

He pointed to the outboard engine.

"Which is engine Number Two?"

He pointed to the inboard engine.

"Which is engine Number Two?"

A New Mission in Life

He looked at me, a bit surprised, and again pointed to the inboard engine.

"Which is engine Number One?" ...

I drilled him again and again until I felt convinced that he fully knew the numbers of the two engines on his side.

We took off and flew in over France and on to target. The flak announced itself shortly after we crossed the German border. Big patterns of purple flak bursts blossomed into the sky. We thundered on through the smoke and the hail of steel.

Suddenly, we were hit. Our aircraft was belted with a tremendous impact and sent staggering up. Then, almost instantly, we plunged down. Oats struggled to maintain control.

"Waist gunner to pilot. Waist gunner to pilot. Fire in Number Two. Fire in Number Two."

That's him, I thought. By God, that's *him!*

"Feather Two, Mac!" Oats yelled.

I pounced on the feathering button and held it in hard. Outside, I could see the rich black smoke streak over the trailing edge of the wing. The blades turned into the wind. I cut power to the engine.

After a few anxious moments, the smoke ceased and the fire was out. We returned safely to Great Britain that day without any further damage.

This simple incident deepened my faith in the guidance of God.

Of great strength and encouragement to me during the autumn months of 1944 was the loyal friendship of Flight Lieutenant David Howell, an officer in the Royal Air Force. I met Dave through his brother, Wing Commander Edward Howell, at the Moral Re-Armament headquarters in London. Dave was a navigator on a Lancaster medium heavy bomber and, like his brother, he was a man of tremendous inner conviction and steadfast faith in God.

On his free nights, Dave would hitch-hike 40 miles to my airbase to see me. For hours we would chat together about the inspiring experiences we had found in our own lives and about our hopes for the world when the war ended. We would listen for direction and talk over our thoughts. "The best way to keep an experience of Christ," Dave would say with a merry twinkle in his eye, "is to give it immediately to someone else."

We began to plan how we might bring an experience of Christ to the men and women we worked with - to our crews, our friends and our families at home. I thought of Oats, Hank, Jimmy Fender and Punchy. How could I share with them the experience I had found?

Simple common sense suggested that if I were to have a life-changing affect on any other person's life, it would mean I would have to accept certain disciplines in my own life which I had heretofore been unwilling to accept. It was plain to see that I could not help anyone be released from the hold of his own bad habits unless I was free of them, myself.

One thing immediately came to mind. ... My pipe.

I had been fond of smoking occasionally. I smoked more or less to create an impression on other people, I suppose.

There were men on our airbase, however, who were addicted to smoking. Some men longed to stop, but couldn't. I had never considered it necessary to cut out such a seemingly harmless habit as smoking until I became passionately interested helping other people.

Therefore, I laid my pipe away, and I have never smoked since.

A revolution was taking place in my nature. Other people's needs were becoming the center of my life instead of my own needs.

A New Mission in Life

But one thing weighed heavily on my mind. It involved a girl.

A few weeks earlier, I had gone down to see my father's brother in the southwestern part of England. Uncle Bill was a doctor. During the days I spent with him at his hospital, I was introduced to a nurse who worked there. Her brother happened to be a first pilot in our bomber squadron. We soon got to talking with each other. Before long, we were having many wonderful times together.

When I got back to base, I found myself thinking about her. I soon began to use every three-day pass to "go see my uncle Bill".

Now that I had decided to live straight in my own life for the sake of other people, I found I was deeply troubled by my relationship with the nurse. In truth, I was actually engaged to a girl back in America. I had carefully concealed this fact from the nurse so that nothing would mar our friendship.

We were on a mission over Germany a few days later. The flak was coming up with terrible accuracy. We watched in horror as plane after plane in our group plunged down from the sky in a train of fire and smoke. Men were dying.

Then, we were hit. I began losing hope. I didn't think we were going to make it back. "St. Peter is really going to give me hell," I thought, "for not being honest with that nurse!" "Oats," I said over the intercom, "if we get back to base, remind me that I've got a letter to write!"

We flew on through the smoke in that sky of death, and somehow managed to limp home and reach ground safely. After debriefing, I immediately wrote to the nurse, and told her the truth. I apologized. I had been selfish and unfair and had deceived her.

I sealed up the letter and mailed it before supper. A wrong relationship was severed, and I felt a free man.

Chapter 7

Reaching Out

The men on the crew soon began to notice a difference in me and were interested. Late one night I was sitting on my bed writing a letter home. There was a knock on the door. It was Sergeant O'Kane, my waist gunner.

"Come in, Punchy," I said.

O'Kane had been a professional boxer in his life before the war. He had fought Sugar Ray Robinson at one point in his career. He was a tough individual and had earned the respect, and occasionally the fear, of many of the men on the crew. We had nicknamed him "Punchy".

I myself had been afraid of Punchy and somewhat divided from him. I had often sensed disgust in his eyes when I had caught him looking at me – there was some deep bitterness which I supposed was due to the fact that he was a sergeant and I was a commissioned officer. Punchy had tried to become a pilot in training, but for some reason never made it. We had never gotten on well together.

Punchy sat for a long time on a box near my bed. I had no idea in the world what he was going to say.

"What's on your mind?" I ventured after a long silence.

Punchy looked me in the eye. "What in the hell was going on up there today?"

We had come through a harrowing day over Germany. We had been hit. But on the way back, I had listened for guidance and God told me what to do step by step. I had lost my fear. Punchy noticed a change in me and had been unable to explain it.

"I don't know, Punchy," I said. "It's hard to describe. About half way back from the bomb run today, it looked so darn hopeless. I was sure we were headed for a ditching in the North Sea. I thought that this time we had surely had it for keeps."

Punchy was studying his boots.

"I was so darn scared," I went on, "that I didn't honestly know what to do. So I started praying."

"Yes, I did too," he said unexpectedly.

"Did you?"

"'Wasn't much of a prayer. All I could remember was, 'Our Father which art in Heaven.' So I kept on saying it over and over again as fast as I could."

I was electrified. Punchy had never talked like this before. He had never even hinted that he had been afraid. But those must have been anxious moments back in the waist turret that day, not knowing fully what our chances were, having to depend entirely on what happened up in the cockpit.

"Where does that come from, by the way?" he asked.

"That's the Lord's prayer, Punchy," I said.

He fell silent again. It had never occurred to me before that this man sitting before me had probably never had any real friends before. I had been afraid of him and had been blind to what had been going on in his heart.

"You know," he finally said, "I've never been to church since I was five." ...

I said nothing. He didn't seem to want an answer.

Suddenly, he looked up at me. "Mac, when I heard your voice over the intercom this afternoon, it got me so damn mad that I forgot about being afraid."

"Why? What did I say?"

"It wasn't what you said," he snapped, "it was the way you said it. You seemed so sure of everything, so relaxed. I couldn't figure you out."

I began to tell Punchy what had happened in my life ... how I had been spoken to very clearly by God, how I had given my life to Him, and how my fear and uncertainty had been completely swept away.

He listened carefully, not saying a word. After I finished, he sat still, examining his boots for a long time.

Finally he got up from the box and went to the door. At the door he grunted something which I supposed was "Good night" ... and then walked off into the darkness. I got up to close the door he had left swinging and caught sight of him as he disappeared around a corner.

I was thrilled. The deep division between Punchy and me had begun to heal. We had started to become friends in the course of ten minutes.

We were having serious trouble with our tail gunner in the air.

Frank, our tail gunner, was from Brooklyn, New York. He wore bottle-thick glasses. In manner, he was quiet and withdrawn. There was a look of fear and intense shyness in his eyes. He neither drank nor smoked and was quite removed from the rest of the crew who did. In the presence of officers, Frank was timid and quiet. I noticed that he could rarely keep his eyes on another person's face.

On one mission, while we were winging high out across the North Sea on our way towards Germany, I gave the order for the tail gunner to test-fire his guns. There was a long pause. I listened for the guns.

"Tail gunner to co-pilot. Tail gunner to co-pilot." Frank's voice was hesitant. "My guns are not working."

Reaching Out

It was an uncomfortable situation to be in, flying towards enemy territory with no protection from the rear.

"Co-pilot to waist gunner." Punchy O'Kane, our waist gunner, was also the armorer of the plane. "Go back and see what's wrong with the tail turret fifty calibers."

O'Kane discovered that the oil was too thick and had frozen. The guns were jammed. It was a simple error that Frank had made in the maintenance of his guns on the ground. It was soon remedied.

A few days later, however, it happened again. This time we were seriously concerned. It was the responsibility of every gunner on the crew to see that his guns were in adequate condition before leaving the ground. The highly complicated mechanism required a great deal of attention and detailed checking prior to take-off. Perhaps Frank had neglected to do this.

Oats and I spoke quite severely to Frank once we were back on the ground. This could NOT happen again. It was a matter of life and death to have protection from the tail position. He was to check his guns thoroughly before every mission from now on.

Frank arrived on the field two days later, determined that nothing should go wrong. We sat in our positions in the ship. Shortly before zero hour I saw the squadron commander in his jeep speeding down the perimeter track.

Suddenly there was a deafening burst of machine-gun fire. Frank's fifty-calibers were blazing out across the field, narrowly missing the jeep.

"What the hell is going on back there?" Oats yelled.

The squadron commander bailed out of his jeep and hit the ground running, headed towards our plane.

There was a deathly silence from Frank in the tail position.

A Pathway through the Sky

The major swung aboard and thundered back through the bombbays. What the devil was going on? Damn near hit the driver of the jeep! Who the hell taught him how to fire a gun? What did he think it was - a toy? How the hell did he ever get into the Air Force?

I could just hear snatches of the fury that was raining down on Frank's head. The major threatened him with ground duty – with *latrine* duty – if it ever happened again. Frank was stone still.

The major leapt off the plane. Moments later we took off for Germany.

This incident clinched it. We would have to find a replacement for Frank. This kind of thing could not be allowed to go on any longer. Frank was a frightened man and was no help to the crew.

He had only been trying to condition his guns. His finger had slipped and had accidentally tripped the trigger. He had been so determined that nothing should go wrong when we reached high altitudes that he had committed the ultimate error of errors on the ground. It seemed that his days of flying were over.

I, too, had been a frightened man. But I had found an answer. My fear left me when I had listened to God and had obeyed Him. A real change had taken place in my nature. Why couldn't the same thing happen to Frank?

In one of my times of listening a few mornings later, I wrote down the impelling thought: "Go on a walk with Frank and tell him everything about yourself. Be absolutely honest with him."

I threw down my pencil. That was impossible! I was Frank's superior officer. It was ridiculous to think of being absolutely honest with *him!* For one thing, it would destroy his confidence in me. It would destroy discipline in the crew.

I argued at length in my own mind. But finally I became quieter.

Reaching Out

God had given me clear direction at moments when my life was in danger. If it was His will for me to be absolutely honest with Frank, it might not harm; it was worth a try

I made up my mind to see Frank the very next day.

We walked for a long ways over country roads together. I told him many things about myself; how fearful I had been in combat; how I used to live through real terror when the flak bursts opened up at high altitudes; how my fear went straight to my stomach and tightened it as hard as a rock. I was afraid of dying. My family and my home were very dear to my heart. I wanted to return to Pennsylvania someday when the war was over. War was hell. I hated it.

I also told Frank many things that I had been ashamed of. I told him about my hopes and dreams. All my life I had been ambitious. I had wanted to be President of the United States. Ever since I was thirteen years old, I had secretly nursed that hope. I had educated myself in the polite but ruthless pursuit of power, prestige and personal advantage. I had compromised my morals to get from others what I wanted.

It was difficult to say all this. But at last I got everything out in the open.

"Frank," I said, turning to him. "I'm sorry I have never before let you know what kind of a guy I am and that I've put up such a front to hide what I was really like."

We walked on silently. The rolling meadows were alive, the smell of harvest hay fresh on the breeze. It was a wonderful afternoon.

"You know," Frank said at length, "there are many things in my life I'm ashamed of too; things I've never told anybody about before."

We stopped and climbed up on an old vine-clad turn-style. Frank began to talk freely. ... Yes, flying *did* terrify him. He wanted to go home too. He told me about a girl he absolutely adored back in the United States; he wrote her no less than three times a day. He told me about his parents; they were in the divorce courts. That hurt. Sometimes he felt his world was going into a tail-spin.

He had been afraid of Oats and me. The day the squadron commander bawled him out, he was not sure whether he wanted to live or die. Somehow it just seemed that he couldn't do *anything* right.

We sat quietly thinking for a long while. I sensed that something new was coming over Frank; his fear was leaving him. I hoped so.

... I had never tried to help another man in this way before.

It was a long time before we climbed down from that old turn-style and walked back to the base.

Not many days later, we were up at 17,000 feet, moving in over the coast of France. We were flying "high squadron" in our bomber group, above the other squadrons and slightly to the right.

From the cockpit, I could see the vast pattern of B-24s below us. The sky was filled with planes.

Suddenly, Frank called in from the tail turret, "Bandits at seven o'clock high!" ... German fighters always attacked from the rear of a formation, picking off the last planes in the group for a kill. "High squadron" was in the most vulnerable position of all. Our bomber group depended on us for defense protection.

"Here they come!" Frank said.

I could hear them. Five ME-109's were screaming down from sun position and coming straight for us.

Frank had been calm and at peace all morning. His guns were working at maximum efficiency and he had given them utmost care and attention. His voice was strong and unhesitating.

Reaching Out

The bomber shook with the vibration of the machine guns. Over the roar of the engines, I could hear the fighters howling down through the sky. Shells were ripping through our fuselage. I prayed.

Frank was still firing, holding his guns on the lead plane.

"Give 'em hell!" Punchy was shouting. "Give 'em hell!"

Suddenly, the lead ME-109 burst into flames and plunged crazily down. A long column of black smoke trailed the fighter through the sky as it hurtled earthward.

A cheer went up through the plane. Frank had gotten his first credit and had disorganized the fighter attack. The fighter squadron soon dispersed.

I smelled gasoline and spun around. Our fuel tanks had been punctured in the fighter attack. It looked like water draining through a sieve. Red gasoline was sloshing around ankle-deep in the bomb-bay. We had to act fast.

"Pilot to bombardier. Pilot to bombardier. Open the bomb-bay doors."

"Roger."

It was a dangerous thing to do. It was equally dangerous to keep a bellyful of gasoline splashing around. Any part of the electrical system, any spark, could ignite the fumes. The plane would explode.

"Easy now. Slowly."

We waited nervously. The smallest spark of friction could mean the end for us.

The doors parted at the center and slowly yawned open. Gasoline was sucked out and flung into our slipstream.

Punchy shrieked. He was getting soaked.

I looked back again. Gasoline was still dripping from the tanks, but in less quantity. The tanks were gradually sealing themselves.

We banked out of formation and turned 180 degrees back towards England. We might just have enough gas to get us back. Everything heavy would have to be thrown overboard.

We dropped our bombs. The aircraft was lifted upwards with a surge of release, and Streicher closed the bomb-bay doors.

"Our hydraulic equipment is out," Oats said.

I looked at the pressure gauge which indicated almost no pressure in the line. Probably it had been punctured. We would have to crank down the landing flaps and the wheels by hand.

We flew onwards towards England. Fortunately, only armor-piercing lead projectiles had struck our plane in the fighter attack. One exploding shell could have touched off a gigantic explosion in our tanks which would have destroyed us all. Again, we had been incredibly lucky.

The commanding officer at our base advised us by radio not to land at our own field; the shorter runway was being used that day due to the direction of the wind. There was a field nearby where the runways were longer.

"Roger," said Oats, putting down the microphone. There were so many darn airfields that it would be hard to find the right one. Our gas was getting terribly low.

We contacted the control tower of the alternate field; then asked our navigator for a course to the approach. Streicher guided us in over the fields of East Anglia ...

Through the haze, I spotted the lay-out of an airfield. Oats banked the plane and came in for his approach. Punchy manually cranked down the flaps and landing gear. We quickly skimmed down over the tree-tops and hedges. Our wheels touched down on the end of the runway.

Suddenly the radio crackled: "Ship on runway! Ship on runway! This is Darky Control tower. You are landing on the wrong runway! You are landing on the wrong runway!"

Darky Control tower? This was not the field we had contacted!

I felt sure we didn't have enough gas to make another pass.

"Ship on runway to Darky," I replied. "We're just back from combat. We're shot full of holes and we aren't going anywhere!"

There was just enough hydraulic power left for application of the brakes. I slowly pressed down on the brake pedal – harder and harder – then with all my might I shoved it down as far as I could. We slowed down at the end of the runway. The plane stopped and we taxied off onto the perimeter track.

As we moved around the track, our Number Three engine coughed and sputtered. Soon it choked and stopped dead.

"My God," Oats whispered. "That's the end of our gas."

Our tanks were dry.

Chapter 8

Assignment to USSTAF

"McLaughry," the colonel said, "there's nothing the matter with you."

I looked into my commanding officer's face, startled and confused. He laughed and slapped me on the back.

I watched him making his way through the confusion of men milling about the dining room, up to the head table where he seated himself with the senior officers.

Oats came up behind me. "What was *that* all about?"

"Darned if I know."

"*You* sure seem to be a pal of the CO!"

"I didn't think he knew I existed," I said. "Why would a commander in charge of hundreds of men pay any attention to me?"

I went through the cafeteria line for my supper, and sat down at my table. It was early March and the warm food tasted better than ever in the chill spring evenings.

Afterwards, I went over to the squadron headquarters for my mail. I walked into the crowded room.

"When are you leaving, Mac?"

I turned around to see who it was. Matthews, the squadron sergeant, was grinning at me from behind the front desk. He was always pulling my leg, old Matthews. Every night he had some new idea up his sleeve.

"Oh, tomorrow, I guess. Maybe the next day!" I sauntered up to the desk, smiling.

Assignment to USSTAF

Matthews took off his reading glasses. "Look, I'm not kidding." He was an excellent straight-faced actor, I thought.

"What do you mean?" I asked, cautious not to appear taken in by his remarks.

"Look at this." Matthews turned around and drew out a long typewritten sheet from a drawer behind him. He handed it to me.

"You've gone to a lot of trouble tonight," I said. "When did you type this up?"

"Go on. Read it."

The type-written sheet was headed: "HEADQUARTERS EIGHTH AIR FORCE". It had been very neatly copied.

"This all looks very impressive," I said.

"Of course."

I read on down the page. There were several orders of the day for different bomber commands. I skipped over them.

Suddenly, I was startled to read my name. "FIRST LIEUTENANT JAMES A. MCLAUGHRY HEREBY RELEASED FROM THE SECOND AIR DIVISION. REASSIGNED TO HEADQUARTERS USSTAF MARCH 12, 1945."

I looked at Matthews. "Is this a joke?"

"No, I swear to God it's not."

The order was signed at the bottom, "BY ORDER OF GENERAL JAMES DOOLITTLE."

There was no doubt about it. This was the genuine article. This was not one of Matthew's pranks.

"Not many guys get orders like that, Mac."

I was shaken and surprised. What was I to do? Where was I to go? What was this all about anyway?

I suddenly remembered the incident at supper with the colonel. He must have known something about this. "That would explain his coming over …"

Matthews stared at me. "Yes sir?"

"Never mind," I said. I turned and walked out of the room, past different groups of men in the entrance hall, hopped on my bicycle and peddled down through the driving rain to Colonel Johnson's quarters. I threw my bike on the grass and raced up to the door.

I knocked. Colonel Johnson appeared. I forgot to salute or to stand at attention. I held out the orders and asked him, "What in the world is all this about?"

Handing him the order, I followed him through the door. He paced into the living room to study it. "Yes," he said at length, "I read this earlier."

"But what does it mean?"

"Just what it says, I guess."

The colonel sat down on a settee in his living room. "I don't know how it came about. General Anderson's headquarters phoned us up today and asked if it would be all right with us to have you reassigned. I said it was all right with me."

I sat down on the arm of the settee. "But … but … why? Where did …"

"Is General Anderson a relation of yours or something?"

"No."

"Is he a friend of the family?"

Assignment to USSTAF

"No sir. I've never even heard of him before." In fact, I had never even *seen* a general before, except at a distance.

The colonel studied on down the pages. Presently he handed the copy of the orders back to me.

"Well, for Pete's sake, whatever you do, don't bring General Anderson around here."

I was just as confused as ever. I didn't know where the order had originated or why it had come. I didn't know what to do or where to go. I didn't even know what the initials USSTAF stood for. Moreover, I had no idea where I was to find General Anderson's headquarters or how to get there.

"Do you know where USSTAF headquarters are, sir?"

"Oh, they are somewhere down in London, I think." The colonel paused. "Now let me think. Maybe they have moved over to France by now."

That was no help.

"You'd better go down to the Administration Headquarters and get your papers checked out," the colonel said. "They will probably have some idea of where USSTAF headquarters is located."

"Thank you, sir." I got up slowly.

"If *they* don't know, go into London and ask at General Eisenhower's Headquarters there."

I gulped. It all seemed so unreal, so utterly fantastic, so sudden. It was like some kind of a dream – or night-mare.

I walked outside and got on my bike.

As I peddled down to the base administration headquarters through the darkness, I remembered that I had not behaved very well

68

A Pathway through the Sky

before my senior officer. I blushed to think that I had not saluted him either on arrival or departure. I had not even stood at attention. In fact, I had walked right into his house without any invitation and immediately had sat down on the arm of his settee.

No one at the administration headquarters seemed to be clear about where the USSTAF headquarters were. I decided to make my way to London and inquire at General Eisenhower's headquarters as the colonel suggested.

I got my papers checked out and was paid up to date. My squadron commander arranged to have me flown down to London the next morning on one of the newly-maintenanced bombers. One of the crews would be putting in time on a new engine. I was to be ready to leave at 0930 hours.

That night I packed all my belongings in my foot-locker. I had accumulated a great deal of odd stuff during my months on base. I would have to leave many things behind.

Oats and Hank Streicher came in to see me. ... It was going to be hard to leave the crew, I thought. We had been together for so many months. We had gone through so much together. Our experiences in combat had drawn us very close.

I went around calling on each of them – Jimmy Fender, Frank, old 'Punchy', Bill Flesey, George Judd and all the rest.

I walked back to my Nissen hut alone. I was going to miss them all. Where in the world could you find a better bunch of guys? This was such a sudden move. There had been no time to prepare for it.

The next day, I was flown down to London.

When I arrived at the London airfield, I immediately reported in at the control tower, and discovered that an order had come through for me. I was to remain at the field and to await further instructions.

Assignment to USSTAF

"What does this mean?" I asked the control tower officer.

"I'm sorry, sir, that's all I can tell you at the moment."

I was exasperated. "This order must have come from somewhere. Where's it from?"

"It came from your own bomber base, sir."

I went over to a phone and called my base to clarify my orders. The reply was equally vague. They could give me 'no further information'. I hung up the phone in dismay.

"Sir, may I suggest that you go down to the mess and have some lunch? I'll get in touch with you directly when further instructions come in."

There was nothing else to do. I went downstairs, had lunch, and afterwards slept on a cot in the control tower. The hours passed by.

Eventually, towards mid-afternoon, I was ordered out to the landing strip to meet "a plane" that was just landing. I grabbed my foot-locker, went outside, and hopped in a jeep. A sergeant drove me out to the field. A small Beechcraft executive-type plane was pulling in at a hardstand.

The pilot cut both engines and climbed down out of the cock-pit. I saw that he was a captain, and promptly drew myself to attention, remembering painfully my negligent informality of the night before.

"Hop in, Mac!" he shouted warmly. "She's all yours!"

She's all yours! What did that mean?

As the captain walked up to me, I saluted him smartly.

"Howdy," he said, sticking out his hand. "I am Captain Walker, General Anderson's personal pilot. How do you like her?" he said, pointing towards the Beechcraft.

A Pathway through the Sky

"It's a very nice plane, sir." I was still confused.

"Come on. We've got to get going," he said.

I followed him up to the plane and swung my foot-locker aboard. We climbed in and got strapped into the seats. Captain Walker started the engines and taxied the plane over to the end of the runway.

"This will seem something like a kite to you after flying a bomber!" he shouted.

The noise of the engines increased to a roar and we moved off down the runway, quickly gathering speed. Before we had gone a third of the distance down the strip, we had taken off into the air.

"Fantastic!" I shouted.

"It's a great little plane," the captain replied. "Very quick on the controls."

He banked the plane over in a sharp turn and we headed out across the fields. We flew low over the countryside, heading eastwards towards the Channel. Within half an hour, we had crossed the coastline.

I could contain my curiosity no longer. Finally, I turned to Captain Walker, "Could you tell me, sir, where are we going?"

Captain Walker threw his head up in the air and roared with laughter. "Oh, I'm sorry. I thought you knew." He quickly unraveled a detailed map. "We're going to a little town north of Paris. Right here," he said, pointing to it with his finger. "It's called St. Germain-en-laye. It's where the Headquarters of the United States Strategic and Tactical Air Forces are located."

"Oh." I leaned back. At least *one* mystery was solved.

The captain brought the plane down very low over the water. We

Assignment to USSTAF

skimmed close to the tops of the waves as we came closer and closer to the coast of France. At the last minute, he yanked the nose up and we roared up over the cliffs. We continued at tree-top level across the fields of Normandy, scaring cows.

... It was the first time I had really been able to see France.

Eventually we arrived in the vicinity of Paris. The captain flew low over small hamlets and villages north of the city. A lone winding road led over the gently rolling countryside and through the dark pine forests. We followed it.

Soon we came upon a small airstrip which had been cleared out of the forest. It was just long enough for a small plane to land. The captain brought the plane down on the earth runway, turned at the end and pulled to a stop.

The field obviously had been cleared only a few months before hand. Some of the tree stumps had not yet been removed from the landing strip periphery, and tall grass had sprung up at the edge of the forest.

Captain Walker took me directly to Major General Frederick Anderson's office in the headquarters building. It was an area of school buildings, formerly a girls' private school, which had been occupied by the Air Force. We walked up the stairs and through the door.

I was quickly introduced to the staff. Suddenly my eyes fell on a face I knew. Colonel Bob Snyder was standing by a large desk, grinning broadly, his hand outstretched to greet me. I was delighted and relieved to find someone I knew. Perhaps, at last, the fantastic mystery of the last twenty-four hours could be solved.

I had not known the Colonel very long. We had met for a short while in London at the home of a mutual friend. In the informal atmosphere of a family, we had talked together. I had told him in the course of our conversation about my adventures as a bomber pilot and of the experiences I'd had. I had begun to talk with him about the experience I had discovered of listening to God daily for direction.

This had been our only contact with each other. Since that conversation I had not seen him, nor had I heard of him.

"Come on into my office," Colonel Snyder said. I followed him through a small door. He showed me to a chair.

"Jim, it's good to see you again," he said warmly.

"This is quite a surprise, sir. I'm glad to see someone I know."

The colonel laughed. "Yes, the last hours must have been quite an experience for you. You must have a lot of questions."

I smiled. "Yes sir."

The colonel walked over and sat down in a large swivel chair behind his desk. "Well, it's really not such a deep mystery, Jim. Let me explain."

He leaned forward on the desk. "I was transferred not long ago to General Anderson's office here in St. Germain. Before that, I was in London. The transfer came not long after our talk together.

"One of the first things that General Anderson asked of me was to find him a personal pilot. I remembered the talk we had had together, and all you told me. You naturally came to mind. So I put the order through yesterday and ... "

"... and here I am."

"And here you are. We're glad to have you."

It was almost unbelievable. I was to fly as the personal pilot of a general!

"But, what about the fellow who flew me here from London?" I

Assignment to USSTAF

asked. "Captain Walker? Isn't he General Anderson's personal pilot at present?"

"Yes. He's finished his tour of duty and is returning to the States."

It still seemed too fantastic to believe. One day, a co-pilot on a bomber crew; the next day, the personal pilot of a general.

"Sir ... I – I don't know how to thank you for this."

"Jim, I wouldn't have done it unless I felt that you were the man for the job. Besides, I feel that the things we talked about together that night in London will stand you in good stead around here."

"I remember that talk, sir."

"If there's anything we need these days, it is the guidance of the Voice of God. We need His direction and leading in rebuilding the world when this war is at last over."

"... It's a great opportunity, sir."

"Well, two of us are better than one," the colonel said. "We can fight this battle together now." He leaned back in his chair. "We may have a chance under God to work miracles just like the ones you had in combat."

"If we are going to build a *lasting* peace, sir, we will need them."

"You must meet the General, Jim!" the colonel said, getting up from his chair.

"I'm ashamed to say it," I confessed, "but I had never even heard his name before I left the base this morning."

Colonel Snyder laughed. "Oh, he's one of the men who runs this outfit they call the US Army Air Forces. His official title is Deputy Commanding General for Operations, United States Strategic and Tactical Air Forces in Europe."

I suddenly felt very small and way out of my depth.

"Don't worry," he said, putting his hand on my shoulder, "you'll find him one of the friendliest guys you ever met. He's very easy to get along with."

I got up and followed the colonel out of the room.

Major General Frederick L. Anderson, Jr.,
Deputy Commanding General for Operations,
United States Strategic and Tactical Air Forces in
Europe - 1945

Chapter 9

Pilot for a General

During the next days, I began to get acquainted with my new surroundings.

General Anderson, to my relief, was all that Colonel Snyder had described him to be. Although I was awed at first by his rank and position, he seemed to ignore the fact that I was his subordinate and inferior. He treated me more as though I were a fellow pilot and a friend. I made up my mind to serve him as selflessly and as thoughtfully as God would show me.

The Beechcraft which I flew was a beautiful airplane. The cabin boasted many windows and a spacious interior. The seats were very comfortably upholstered.

After months in heavy cumbersome bombers, I found the small plane extremely maneuverable and spry. It was all I had longed for, all one could hope for as a pilot.

I began to fly the General on many short trips to various airfields in France and Belgium, as well as to advance points behind the front lines. He was frequently required to confer with General Carl Spaatz, Commander of USSTAF, at his advance headquarters in Reims. Several times we made short flights across the Channel to England, and back again to Paris. The general's responsibilities called him to conferences or missions of a highly specialized nature every few days.

As the war neared its end in Europe, several senior officers of the Air Force were called to Cannes in the southern part of France to confer with General "Hap" Arnold, Commanding General of the Army Air Forces around the world. Many problems had to be sorted out.

Once military victory was achieved in Europe, the United States would have to direct all the attention of her combined armed forces to

A Pathway through the Sky

winning the war against Japan. The reallocation of personnel had to be considered. Thousands would be transferred from the European theater to the Pacific.

As well as personnel, tons and tons of equipment would have to be dealt with. Bombers would have to be flown to the States from bases in Italy, Britain and France. There were innumerable details to be discussed in the gigantic shift.

The day for the conference drew near. General Anderson informed me that we were to take off at 9:30 on a Monday morning from the air strip at St. Germain.

I got the plane fueled and ready for the flight.

The day of our flight dawned cloudless, the sky a deep rich blue. Spring was in the air. It was one of those days when all the world seemed to be bursting to life.

We turned up-wind at the end of the earth airstrip, the General at the controls. The trees at the far end of the field seemed to be shimmering with the waves of heat rising from the ground. There was ever so slight a breeze.

The General pushed the throttles forward and we gathered speed and moved down the runway. It was hot. Towards the end of the runway, the plane picked itself up into the air and climbed out over the trees. We banked over to the south.

"What's the course, Mac?"

I pulled out a large map of France on which the course was drawn. Our plane was rocking in the warm drafts of air rising from below.

"We'll have to fly due south, sir, to skirt around those mountains," I said. "Then, about three hundred miles down, we take a diversion to the east. We should reach Nice, which is near Cannes, in about three and a half hours, roughly."

"No, no, Mac. That's not the way to go," the General replied. "It's not direct enough."

"What do you mean, sir?"

"Well, let's make a straight line for Nice." The General drew a rough line with his finger straight across the map.

"But sir, there are very high mountains in the way if we go straight. We'll never climb over them in this plane."

"Well then," the General said, "let's go through them!"

He shifted the propellers to a coarser pitch. There was a smile on his face.

I grew apprehensive.

After about three quarters of an hour, we flew in over the foothills of the Alps. The view was exquisite. The sun shone down on the sparkling snow on towering peaks in the distance. The mountain-tops were etched against the sky, strong and majestic.

We flew straight on towards the mountains ahead. Soon we were skimming over high valleys and in through narrow passes and *cols*. Black rugged ribs of rock protruded through the snow and ice of the higher peaks. The cliffs seemed treacherous and unscalable. We wove in and out among mountain-tops, flying frighteningly close. ... Then, the mountains passed behind us.

We flew on over the rolling countryside. ... Two hours later we landed at Nice and drew up to the side of the field. The General cut the engines.

"We made good time, Mac." He looked at his watch. It was just a few minutes after noon.

"This field seems sort of deserted," I said. There was no sign of a reception committee at the small terminal building. "There certainly should be a staff car here."

"Are you sure this is the right field?" the General asked.

"There is no field marked at Cannes, sir. I thought this was where we were supposed to come."

"Talk to the control tower and ask them if they know anything."

"The control officer speaks French, sir."

"Do you?"

I shook my head. I hadn't been able to make out his landing instructions.

"We'll go to Cannes, then," the General said. "There must be some other field we don't know about."

The General pulled the plane around and we quickly took off.

There would certainly be some kind of staff car to pick up the General at the airport we were looking for. Perhaps a strip had been recently cleared in the vicinity of Cannes. We would have to fly at low level and explore.

We flew directly for Cannes and came down over the roof-tops.

Presently, we found a small field just outside of the city. It was a grass strip. The chalk markers on the runway were just barely visible from the air.

We quickly landed and climbed out. Here a staff car was awaiting the general's arrival. He was welcomed and quickly driven into the city for the conference.

Later that day, I had been to Marseilles to refuel the Beechcraft and was returning to Cannes. I skimmed low over the sparkling waves of the bay on my way back, drinking in the warm sunshine of the afternoon and the thrill of flying all alone.

I noticed a group of American cruisers riding at anchor nearby and swooped down to get a closer look. A few sailors waved from the after-deck of one of the ships as I made a long circle over the water. I rolled gently up on one wing and headed on.

It was perfectly exhilarating to soar through the air so free, so unattached, so light and strong!

I pulled the nose up and climbed quickly to a thousand feet, leaving the ships behind in the distance.

That night, I went in to supper, feeling refreshed by the wonderful afternoon I had spent. My appetite had been sharpened and I piled food high on my plate.

Towards the end of supper, General Spaatz's personal pilot joined me for coffee.

"I hear you were out buzzing the United States Navy this afternoon!" he said.

I looked at him inquisitively. "How did you know about that?"

"Oh, I found out."

"Where?"

"Well, as a matter of fact, you had quite an audience – General Spaatz, General Arnold, General Anderson ... "

"You're kidding!"

"No, no! They all started talking about it. They watched you sweeping and diving around the bay, scaring up the Navy boys."

I felt myself getting red. "Where were they?"

"Swimming on the beach."

"And you were with them?"

"Yes. General Arnold recognized that it was a Beechcraft and turned to General Anderson. 'That's your pilot, isn't it?' he asked General Anderson. "Then they all watched you for a while, trying to figure out who it was."

"Did General Anderson say anything?"

"He stuck up for you. 'No, no' he said 'that's not McLaughry. McLaughry wouldn't do anything like that.'"

"What did the others say?"

"They couldn't figure out who it was after that, so they went right on swimming."

I breathed a sigh of relief.

"You know, I bet General Anderson still won't believe it was you out there!" He slapped me on the back, roaring with laughter.

I felt deeply embarrassed.

As the weeks wore on, the General began to give me more and more minor responsibilities and errands. I became his virtual aide-de-camp as well as his pilot, and learned how to operate with him at his right hand when we were on the ground.

In my morning times of quiet, I would listen for direction from God. I received thoughts with simple clarity and straightforwardness. I had ideas on how to prepare the cabin of the Beechcraft so that it would be more comfortable for the General. It meant making sure that there was some kind of food aboard and that the most recent newspaper would be conveniently located on the table. I also provided maps and other small items which I would not have had the

Pilot for a General

imagination to supply without the creative source of guidance.

I took my responsibility to the General very seriously.

Once, when he was in close conference with General Spaatz at the headquarters in Reims, he sent a message out to the plane asking for his briefcase. The sergeant-at-arms arrived at the ship and asked me for it. I went back into the cabin.

Suddenly I had the thought, "No! Don't give it to the sergeant. Take it yourself!"

It was a strong and compelling idea, the very kind that I had learned from experience was so important to obey. So I took the briefcase and went to the door.

"Thank you, sir," said the sergeant, holding out his hand.

"That's all right," I replied, "I'll take it."

I jumped down and strode across the tarmac to the old school building where the headquarters was located. The sergeant-at-arms followed at a few paces.

We went in through the door and down a long hall. The generals were conferring in a small room at the end. I quietly opened the door and walked in, past the guard, and over to General Anderson. When he had the briefcase safely in his hands, I withdrew outside to wait.

It had been a simple precautionary measure. But it was because of my obedience to thoughts such as these that the General began to rely on me more and more for responsibilities as an aide-de-camp.

In late April, I accompanied General Anderson on a secret mission to Sweden. His purpose was to find out quietly what Sweden might do to help the Allies at the end of the war. Since the Nazi presence was still very strong in Stockholm, we had to be particularly cautious about our movements and our personal security. When we were out in the streets, we dressed as civilians. I acted as a bodyguard to the general, and carried a 45 automatic.

The General interviewed many people at the highest levels of the Swedish government during this visit. As gifts, he carried packages of oranges and grapefruit to interviews – selected instead of liquor because citrus fruits were so scarce during the war.

At one point, General Anderson gave me a briefcase of papers, and said if they fell into the wrong hands, it could change the way the war ended. With such a directive, I guarded those papers day and night, and slept with a pistol beside my bed. I would sit outside his room in the Grand Hotel while he rested, and quietly kept an eye on things.

We were fortunate to witness Sweden's First of May celebration, just a week before VE-day. As a neutral nation, Sweden's capital had never been bombed. For those of us who had been in England and France during the war, it was quite a shock to see a city all lit up. The bonfires and festivities made for a gala day.

If I had not known about guidance, I would have done my daily tasks for the General selfishly and unimaginatively. It was guidance that gave me freedom and creative thoughtfulness for my superior officer. I became alert and sensitive to his needs at all times.

Thus, I began to know for the first time the real joy and satisfaction of serving another person instead of living selfishly for myself, as I had done all my life. God asked me to give everything of myself for the General's sake. In obeying that task, I found an inner peace and happiness such as I had never before experienced.

Chapter 10

Trip through the Land of the Dead

In mid-April, 1945, General Anderson informed me that we would take a week's journey through the bombed-out target areas of Germany. The trip would help provide important data in the evaluation and appraisal of air-power in the war.

As Deputy Commanding General for Operations, General Anderson had been the most responsible under General Spaatz's leadership in deciding which targets were to be hit, whether oil refineries, railroad yards, ball-bearing plants, or vital war production industries. By visiting different war-targets, he would be able to evaluate the amount of damage done, and thereby would be able to assess the effectiveness of the various bombing missions for which he had been responsible.

This was to be a significant trip for me, as well. I had been one of the bomber pilots who had actually taken part in the bombing raids over Germany. I would see vividly for the first time what had happened as a result of our bombing.

We took off from the small airstrip in the woods at St. Germain at 2:30 on the afternoon of April 17th, flying straight to Frankfurt in southern Germany. We traveled together with a C-47 which was carrying two jeeps for our ground transportation within occupied Germany.

At 4:00 p.m., we crossed the Rhine. Below me, I saw the verdant vine-clad terraces, rich green with the early spring rains. It was startlingly beautiful, almost unreal.

Half an hour later, we flew in over Bingen, a small town south of Frankfurt, at about 800 feet. It had been hit hard by the bombing raids. Stretched out beneath our wing were the railroad yards, torn and tattered, gutted almost beyond repair. The railroad bridge had been destroyed. Giant steel girders lay twisted in the moving currents of the river.

A Pathway through the Sky

The neighboring city of Mainz was in ruins. We flew low over the hulks of former factories. Rubble marked the sites of once-thriving industries. Only an occasional smoke stack pointed a charred finger to the sky to mention the erstwhile presence of some great mill or foundry.

It was gray, dark and bleak below us. Not one house appeared habitable. Death and despair seemed to curl up with the traces of smoke from the remains of the city.

Frankfurt had been devastated. I searched down from my cockpit window to find one erect building, one undamaged bridge. Everything had been swept down in the fury of the war. Nothing had been unaffected.

The main landing field at Frankfurt, formerly a large German air terminal, had been destroyed. It was impossible to attempt a landing there.

We brought the Beechcraft down on a small fighter air-strip just outside the city. The C-47 followed shortly and pulled around behind us. The general's jeep was unloaded from the plane, and he was quickly driven into the city for the night.

My engineer and I, and the crew of the C-47, spent the night at the fighter strip. Our supper was served infantry style, out under the sky. We got to talking with some of the pilots and ground-crews.

"Have you guys been here long?"

"Oh, about three or four weeks," replied one of the pilots.

"We moved in pretty well on the tail of the infantry," said another.

"Are things pretty quiet now?"

"Yes, the Germans don't seem to have much of an Air Force any more. One or two fighters, but they don't give us much trouble."

"If we want trouble," said Bill, one of the pilots, "we go out and hunt for it!"

"What do you mean?" I asked.

"Well, the boys go out about four or five times a day to help clear out tank and artillery positions for the infantry. Mostly low-level stuff. Skip bombing and strafing."

In the distance, I heard some machine-gun fire. There were a few short bursts and then it died away again. I looked around in the direction it was coming from. Most of the men seemed to be unperturbed.

The sky was suddenly lit by a brilliant flare, arcing into the air.

"What's that?" I asked.

"Oh, there are some jerries holed up in a pocket in the woods. They've been firing all day."

"Those must be some of the last," said Hank, a ground-crew chief. "Some of those folks just won't give up."

Bill walked over to the edge of the tarmac. "They've sure taken a beating. I wonder what keeps them going."

"I guess they figure they don't have anything to live for now," said Hank. "They might as well die fighting."

Bill turned around. "I don't know. Maybe they feel they do have something to live for. Maybe *that's* why they keep fighting."

"Is there much fighting still going on in the city?" I asked.

"See for yourself," Bill said. "there's nothing much left in the city."

"A lot of people must have died during the bombing there."

"Yes, a thousand were killed in one bombing raid."

A Pathway through the Sky

I looked at Bill, dumbfounded. "A thousand? What happened?"

"The warning signal never went off, they say. It broke down just before the planes came over. Everyone was out in the streets when all hell was breaking loose. There was a hellaciously big fire – wiped out most of the city."

"You know," said Hank, "there were probably a lot of people killed who never wanted a war. Probably hundreds hated Nazism and all it stood for, but were just forced to fight."

"Like that German pilot who landed here the other day," said Bill.

"A German pilot landed here?"

"Yes. He brought his ME-109 with him – all broken up and shot full of holes. He had a rough time trying to convince us that he was here on friendly business."

"The anti-aircraft crews gave him Merry Christmas as he came down over the field. They just about got him, too."

"Where was he from?" I asked.

"Oh, from some fighter group over on the eastern front," Bill said. "They were gradually running out of fuel supplies at his fighter base. They were sending out fewer and fewer planes. Whole squadrons were being grounded simply because there wasn't enough gas to keep them in the air.

"But that wasn't the end of the war for them. Fighter pilots were being inducted into the infantry and sent to the front lines to fight the Russians. ... This guy took off late one night and flew straight across the lines here to Frankfurt."

"Getting out while the getting was good, huh?"

Bill laughed. "I guess he had no more hankering for the infantry than I do!"

Trip through the Land of the Dead

That night, I slept on the ground underneath the wing of the Beechcraft. The night was cold and windless. As I dozed off, I could hear the machine guns rattling away in the pocket of the woods, not many miles away.

I thought of the soldiers behind those guns. Something inside them kept them fighting even though the war was nearly over. They would not give up. They would not let themselves be taken over

During the next five days, we flew on over most of the larger cities of Germany – Nurnberg, Magdeburg, Hannover, Dortmund, Essen, Cologne, Bonn. We flew at roof-top level, surveying the damage of the war. Everywhere it was the same. Homes were burned, cities smashed, industries destroyed. Our eyes grew accustomed to the sight. It was no longer uncommon to see nothing standing over fifteen feet high. As if the elements had turned their furies across the face of the earth, everything had been flung to the ground without mercy.

Germany was a nation in utter ruins. Proud cities no longer existed. It was a ghastly picture of man's savage hatred unleashed on his fellow man.

We took off on the morning of April 20th, heading eastward towards Leipzig. The city at that time was still very close to the front lines. We were informed that fighting was still going on in the streets.

As we flew closer, I noticed a heavy pall of smoke hanging over the entire city. Most of the central part of Leipzig had been smashed by attack bombers. Buildings had crumpled to the ground and there were mountains of rubble everywhere. Mighty structures stood hollow, gutted.

We brought the plane down low, flying over the few standing steeples and towers. The grayness of the smoke was lit by intermittent explosions. Fires were blazing in various sectors of the city, spewing black cottony clouds of smoke into the sky. Brilliant bursts of

A Pathway through the Sky

machine-gun fire flashed beneath us.

General Anderson said, "If you see them start to shoot at us, Mac, we'll take off out of here."

I nodded. I was none too eager to explore further into the city. Our plane was unarmored and had no shrapnel or bullet shielding. A few shells from a sniper's rifle could bring us down.

After a few minutes, we banked west and headed back for the airfield outside the city. We landed and drove into the city by jeep.

In the General's appraisal of the effect of air power in the war, he was particularly concerned with the effectiveness of our bombing raids in halting production in Germany's vital war industries. Thousands of American lives had been lost in the skies during the bombing raids. Planes had gone down by the score. Had it been worth the cost in men and materiel?

During our trip through Germany, we made several trips by jeep to investigate the damage that had been done to various factories. Thus it was, on our fourth day, that we visited the famous underground factory for the V-1 and V-2 missiles at Nordhausen. It was an experience that left a deep impression on me.

The entrance to the underground factory was inconspicuous enough. Outside there were a few pre-assembled parts, a scattering of oil drums and crates. A solitary road and a railway line led through a yawning opening in the side of a low hill.

We followed the tracks through the opening and down through the semi-darkness. Large ventilating ducts hung from the damp stone ceiling of the tunnel. We passed by a barracks area, a mess hall and an infirmary. The underground facilities were easily sufficient for the entire factory staff.

We came upon long assembly lines for the production of the ramjet V-1's, commonly known as the dreaded "buzz-bombs" that had struck terror into so many hearts. There was a second assembly line for the mass production of the V-2 ballistic missile. Cross-shafts connected the two main assembly lines. There was a total of 28 kilometers of underground area utilized for missile production.

In the dim lighting of those shadowed underground caverns, the shapes of the gigantic V-2 rockets made me shudder. They seemed dark, mutinous, deadly, almost like silent ogres awaiting their signal to plunder, kill and destroy. The gleaming tubing of the rocket engines, assembled in long rows, seemed diabolical – a sinister sorcery in steel, a tangled maze of shining metal swept together by the demagogues of the underworld, a world of half-light, half-truths, half-men.

From the bowels of the mountain, the colossal rockets were slowly rolled out. A locomotive hauled trains of rockets down the track, out of the tunnel, into the light of day. They were prepared for launching. The earth would shake with the thunder of ignition and blast off, and they would rise into the air, first slowly, then faster and faster until at last they would grow so small that no eye could longer follow them.

My mind raced back to a day several months earlier when, flying in formation towards Germany, I had noticed a strange shape rising from the far horizon. It was climbing through about 20,000 feet with a short streak of vapor trailing beneath it. As it got to our altitude, it had suddenly accelerated and vanished straight up into the sky. It seemed virtually ghost-like to all of us.

Only weeks later, we began hearing reports of the new "secret weapon" of the Germans and of the fearful effect it was having in the bombing of London.

The immense proportions of the underground factory struck me with awe. The Germans had advanced scientifically with fantastic speed. On various drawing boards were spread the blueprints of missiles. Charts showed that production had been well on the up curve. Had the Germans been spared a few months, the tide of war might have turned in their favor.

"It was an error in their calculations," General Anderson said as we moved out of the tunnel. "If the Germans had equipped themselves with V-2's earlier, we might be fighting our way through the ruins of London or New York."

The General talked more as we drove back to the airfield. He felt that the Germans had put too much faith in fighters. By the time they had switched to missile production, it had been too late.

We drove out onto the airstrip and pulled up beside the C-47. The General turned to me as he climbed out of the jeep. "You know, Mac, sometimes I am persuaded that the Almighty had a hand in this war."

We walked over to the Beechcraft.

One thing was for sure, I thought. We needed the hand of the Almighty more than ever now so that such a tragedy would never happen again to humanity.

Chapter 11

Is There an Answer to War?

It was our last morning in Germany and the Beechcraft was low on fuel. There was no gasoline available at the Weimar airfield where we had landed.

I talked it over with the pilot of the C-47. We decided it would be best to siphon some gas from the tanks of the transport into the tanks of the Beechcraft.

"The immediate problem is to find a length of hose long enough to do the trick. You don't happen to have one on board, do you?"

The pilot shook his head. We looked around the field for a while unsuccessfully.

Towards mid-morning, two officers of the C-47, my engineer and I piled into a jeep and set out for the heart of the city in quest of some rubber hose. Our driver drove at high speeds through the narrow streets, swerving precariously around the bomb-holes and jagged craters in our way.

In one sector of the city, we saw long lines of German prisoners of war seated on a stone wall, guarded by three young American MP's. Their faces were blank and expressionless. Various ones were smoking disconsolately. Others were brooding, studying the ground and gazing into the distance.

I had never seen such complete disillusionment on the faces of men before. The "big idea" for which they had given everything was now shattered. The brave hopes of yesteryear had proved to be meaningless and ineffectual – shimmering castles in the air. Their world laid smoking in ruins, stinking with the smell of death and decay, smashed into ugly heaps of debris. They had been defeated and there was no longer anything to live for.

We turned a corner and sped up a small alley. Two newly released

A Pathway through the Sky

French prisoners were standing on the corner, begging a lift.

"Let's pick them up," I said to the driver.

We screeched to a halt. They walked over and gratefully climbed on to the back of the jeep. "Hang on," someone shouted as we dug out from the curb. Our jeep bounced through the narrow cobbled streets and around a corner on to a main street.

"Do you speak English?" I inquired.

"Yes," one of them smiled pleasantly. He was taller than his companion and by his looks, a few years his senior.

Both men looked lean, gaunt and hungry as though they had not been adequately fed for months.

"Where is your home?" I shouted back.

"Alsace – in the north of France."

"You'll be going back soon, now that the war is nearly over, eh?"

A smile stole over his face. It was as though the idea had not yet occurred to him. "Yes," he replied. "First to Paris."

"Paris? That's where we've just come from."

"Is that so?"

He looked at his friend. "Two days ago we never thought we would make it back."

"What do you mean?" I asked.

"My friend and I were working in a factory near here. We were slave laborers. The Germans treated us badly. We had very little food. We worked all day. Many died. We never thought we would see France again."

Is There an Answer to War?

"But, why?"

"We were to be executed."

"What for?" asked the navigator. "What was the reason?"

"I don't know," he said, shrugging his shoulders. "It is impossible to explain. Yesterday was to be the day. They were going to kill us all. They had killed many of our friends." He glanced at the ruins of a small church nearby. There was no emotion in his eyes – just a deep tiredness. His face was serious and intent.

We noticed many such recently-released slave laborers wandering about in the streets, French, Poles and Russians, all scantily clad and starving. The war had left its hollow mark in men's eyes as well as in the ruined buildings about us. They had seen enough of war, enough of death, almost enough of life. If only there was some hope, some tangible assurance for the future, some knowledge that the same mistakes would never be made again.

We dropped our passengers and continued our search for a length of hose.

Near Buchenwald, we saw a long row of two-door garages, built in a single-storey block. It seemed a logical place to find a length of hose. We swung in at the entrance and drove up the gravel driveway to the administration building. It was deserted.

I jumped down from the jeep to try the door of the first garage. It did not budge.

"Come on, Mac, a little muscle there," the navigator jeered.

"Seems to be locked," I said, trying harder.

The others climbed down from the jeep and came over for a look. One of them studied the hinges. "Say, take a look at this," he said.

"What?"

A Pathway through the Sky

"These hinges. They're fake. They're solid pieces of iron."

I felt them with my hand. Sure enough. They were cleated tightly to the wall.

The navigator was down at the next door. "This is fake too. ... They're *all* fake."

We followed him down the line, studying similar doors which had been fastened to the wall, giving the building the appearance of a long ten-car garage.

"I wonder what this place is anyway," I said. It was a curious building. If it was not a garage, what was it?

"Let's try to get in," the navigator said.

"There's no entrance from the front; let's try the side."

I went around the left side of the building and found a small doorway. I tried it. It opened. We all went into the dark interior.

"Phew! What a smell!" I heard an officer from the C-47 say. It was almost suffocating. There was an acrid, sour odor in the air. We groped through the darkness until we came upon a large room with a skylight up in the roof from which cold dull light was flooding.

"Holy ---- !! Take a look at that!" the navigator said.

In the corner of the room, there was a mountain of discarded clothes – jackets, shirts, trousers, underwear, shoes, hats and all varieties of used clothing.

"I wonder who all those clothes belonged to?" he whispered.

"Come on, let's go further." I found another small door leading from the other side of the room, swinging open on its hinges. We continued on behind the navigator and entered what looked like a huge shower room. The floor was concrete, and various plumbing

Is There an Answer to War?

fixtures protruded from the walls.

It was dark and quite hard to see. We examined the pipes and faucets, still searching for a length of hose.

Suddenly it dawned on me.

"This is no ordinary shower room," I said.

"What do you mean?" the navigator asked.

"Do you see this?" I pointed to a nozzle in the side of the wall.

"Yes. What about it?"

"That was used for gas."

The two other officers quickly came over. We studied the nozzle closely and discovered several others nearby.

"That's what it is, all right," said one of the officers. "This is no shower room. It's a gas chamber."

"That explains all those clothes in the next room," I said.

"Probably people were brought in, actually believing they were going to have a shower," the navigator said slowly.

"It certainly wouldn't take long for the mixture of steam and gas to do its work."

"No wonder there's a false front to this building," I said. "They certainly wouldn't want anybody to know what was going on in here."

We explored through the building, deeply appalled by what we saw. The brutality and outrage of it struck deep into my heart. Hundreds, perhaps thousands, had met their death within these walls. I had read about the Buchenwald 'killing factories' in the newspapers. I had certainly never expected to see them. By accident we had walked right into one of the most notorious gas-chambers in

A Pathway through the Sky

the world.

We walked outside. ... As we drove on through town in the jeep, I was alone with my thoughts. I had seen a sight which would last as a hideous memory for years.

Presently, we found a length of rubber hose suitable for our needs. We turned and headed back for the airport.

A long convoy of trucks passed us on a road leading out of the city; we were forced to park by the side of the ditch as they passed by. A big tank carrier rumbled past us, spattering mud on the side of our jeep. Three Poles were sitting on the curb watching the convoy thunder past with no apparent interest.

"Some of these former slave laborers look as though they won't last much longer without a meal," I said.

"They've been living on next to nothing for months," the navigator said. "What I find so amazing is that any of them are alive at all ..."

We drove on.

As we arrived back at the airport, a young boy saluted us from across the road. With a piercing shriek, he screamed, "Heil Hitler!" and stuck his tongue out at us. Then he scampered away as fast as his legs would carry him, disappearing behind the ruins of an old farmhouse ...

We taxied to the end of the small airstrip, turned into the wind and took off into the afternoon sun. As we flew south towards Paris, we came over beautiful pine-clad hills, reminiscent of the rolling country of western Pennsylvania. Everywhere the glorious greens of spring were blossoming - in trees, on meadows and pastures, all along the brooks and streams. A narrow river wound in and through the valleys.

Spring had returned to the world, and everywhere nature was

rejoicing. I watched our shadow racing across the furrows of the fields. In all the natural glory of the earth that was spread out beneath us, I felt there was something to be learned, something to be taken to heart. The world had cut itself off from its very life-blood. God was in Nature and in Nature was peace and hope and life for all the world.

People needed to turn back to God, the Father, the Supreme Architect of the Universe, if ever they were to build the new world they longed for.

We flew on into the gathering darkness of the evening.

Chapter 12

Returning Home

The war ended in Europe.

Berlin fell before the advancing Russian armies in the East and the Allied Forces in the West. Hitler's successor landed by plane at the Headquarters of the Allied Forces in Reims and, in a small low school building, signed the unconditional surrender of German troops on the continent of Europe.

The last shot had been fired. On this side of the world, at least, military peace had been won.

General Anderson was immediately reassigned to the Pentagon in Washington. As Assistant Chief of Air Staff for Personnel, he was to be in charge of the transfer of all U.S. Air Force personnel back to the United States, and for the reassignment of those needed for the final thrust against Japan.

We prepared to return to Washington at once.

May 8th, 1945, dawned still and quiet. A cool mist was floating over the pine-clad valleys near St. Germain-en-laye and drifting through the trees on the higher slopes. The morning air was fresh and scented with the aroma of freshly plowed earth, of dew-spangled meadows and pastures. Trees were full with the foliage of spring.

The tired old jeep started with a cough. Its lungs had become rusty in the cold, rainy days of winter; it seemed to object to being aroused so early in the morning.

As I headed down the muddy roads towards the airfield, the sun rose from a haze in the east. It was going to be a perfect day. The earth seemed to glisten in the early light. All the world seemed to herald the dawn of Peace.

Returning Home

Now, I reflected, there would be no more armies bleeding across these fields, no tanks, no guns churning the earth, blasting flames and shells through these growing forests, no shrieks from the wounded and dying, no thunder in the skies, no more darkness in the land.

This was a day I would never forget.

I praised God from the bottom of my heart for all the wonders He had showered on me since the day I had decided to obey. Not only had my life been saved again and again since that time, but God had given me a destiny for my life. He had given me a chance to be part of a great adventure of changing men and nations for every last remaining day of my life.

I parked the jeep at the airstrip and walked to the B-17 being fueled on the field. Inside the cabin, there were two nicely made-up beds, comfortable armchairs, a bar and lounge tables. Everything had been well prepared for the General's flight home to America.

General Anderson arrived at the ship. We took off at 10:45 for London and crossed over the English Channel at about midday. A sand-colored haze covered the blue sea. In the distance, I could make out the white chalk cliffs of Dover.

Soon, we were over the open countryside of England again – the rolling fields and meadows of the farming country, the hedgerows and forests.

We spent the night in London, joining in the colossal Victory-Europe celebrations that were going on in the city. Thousands upon thousands jammed together in front of the iron gates of Buckingham Palace, cheering the King and the Royal family.

Behind St. Paul's Cathedral, two powerful searchlights streaked skyward into the night, spreading in a gigantic "V". Lights were on everywhere for the first time in five years. It was a night of jubilation.

The next morning we flew directly to Iceland, landing at Reykjavik Airport in the mid-afternoon. Our Flying Fortress was fueled and checked over by the ground crew. We went in to check the weather.

"Well sir?" said the weather officer without looking up. "What can I do for you?" He was busy studying his charts.

"How does it look between here and Goose Bay?"

"It's bad ... you'll run into a very severe weather front across the central Atlantic," he said. "It's heading east at about 40 miles an hour and was reported last about 200 miles from here."

"Any chance of going around it?"

"Hardly," he said, looking at me over his glasses. "The front extends for 2,000 miles from north to south."

"What altitude does it reach?"

"Probably 20,000 feet. Maybe higher."

28,000 feet was the maximum ceiling of the B-17. If there was no turbulence or precipitation at that altitude, we would be all right.

"Of course," said the weather officer, "you could wait until the storm has advanced to the east of us. It will probably be better flying weather tomorrow."

"The General is in a hurry."

"Perhaps. But the weather waits for no-one."

"Knowing the General, I think he'll only be interested in what kind of weather we'll face – *not* whether we will fly or not. I think we'll probably risk it."

The weather officer folded his maps, looking at me apprehensively. "All right, sir. I wish you luck."

"Thanks." I turned and walked out of the shack.

Returning Home

After a short meal on the ground, we took off into the afternoon sky and climbed steadily up to 25,000 feet. Beneath us, the Atlantic spread as far as the eye could see, ruffled by the west wind, and spotted by small argosies of cottony clouds.

The General went back and stretched out for a nap. Time went by slowly. Towards evening, I noticed a dark line of clouds on the horizon. There it was ... the weather front the ground officer had warned us about. Long banks of cloud stretched far to the south of us. Giant cumulus towered in the north.

As we flew onwards, the sky gradually turned darker and more threatening. Nimbus clouds towered above us, curtaining the copper sun, and finally blinding its friendly eye altogether. Soon we ran headlong into a mammoth wall of angry, scowling clouds and darkness fell. We were swallowed in a single gulp into the midnight darkness of the storm, flying by instruments alone. The ship pitched and heaved violently in the savage wind currents.

Fine ice particles began to sweep over the wing like a dense fog. Often I lost sight of the wing-tips in the whirling confusion outside our window.

We flew on for 20 minutes.

"Mac, look!" the co-pilot shouted over the roar of the engines, pointing beyond me out to our left wing. "Ice!"

It began slowly, forming on the leading edges of our wings and on the air cowlings, a deadly white frost. It grew thicker and our airspeed began to drop.

"Are the deicers on full?" I yelled back.

"Yes sir. On full."

They weren't doing much good. The ice was getting heavier and heavier. Our wings were fast becoming sheeted in white. We would have to go up.

A Pathway through the Sky

"Let's try to climb out of it!" I shouted.

I eased back on the stick and shifted the pitch of the propellers. We climbed steadily until we reached our maximum ceiling.

It was no use. The storm was even more vicious at that altitude. The ice clung on. I glanced at the air-speed indicator. It was low. Dangerously low.

For fifteen minutes, we plunged on through the wild storm, twisting, leaping, crashing down and around in the savage winds. It seemed foolish to try to go farther. I thought it only sensible to turn around and head back to Reykjavik for the night.

I sent word back to the general.

General Anderson walked up to the front of the plane, wiping his eyes. He looked out and studied the thick coating of ice on the wings. Both wings were now an opaque white. He leaned over and gazed at the instrument panel.

"Mac," he said in a sleepy voice, "let me take it." I climbed out of the left seat and helped the General strap himself in.

I was fascinated. The General was not going to let the storm get the better of him. He knew it - and I knew it. He would fight it to the finish.

He put the nose down. We dropped fast through the blinding ice and hail. I watched the altimeter as it fell all the way from 28,000 feet to about 200 feet.

Suddenly, I saw the waves of the Atlantic not far below us. We leveled out over the water and roared onwards over the pitching seas.

The ice began to break loose. Large hunks whipped against the sides of the fuselage. In 10 minutes, the wings were relatively ice-free.

"Can you give me a position?" the General bellowed down to the

Returning Home

navigator.

"Sorry, sir. The radar-radio equipment is no good in this kind of weather. I've been trying to make a contact ever since we got in the storm."

"How far out of Goose Bay are we?"

"Well, judging from the winds we've been hitting, we're about three hours out." ... We flew on.

I began to pray quietly. The Lord had seen me through so many emergencies. He would surely look after us this time.

I sensed the uneasiness in the crew. The hours went by.

"Anything yet?" the General shouted down, keeping his eyes steadfastly on the instruments.

"Not yet, sir."

It got darker. Our navigator was terrified. There was no way of telling our position. The mountains near Goose Bay were uncharted. In this kind of weather, we could easily slam into a mountainside and never be heard of again.

Suddenly, we flew into a giant cavern in the sky. Clouds were still above us and around us ... but far in the distance, through a thin opening in the overcast, I could make out a star.

Radio contact was immediately established with the control tower in Goose Bay. We were 30 miles to the east, and Goose Bay reported clear skies and good visibility. Up until 20 minutes beforehand, the small airfield had been completely weathered in by the storm.

The General brought the plane down low. Soon, the rocky shore line slipped under our wings. After another few minutes, we had the runway in sight. We made our approach. As we came in for our landing, I could see white snow drifts and ice packs piled on either side of the strip. Then, the wheels touched down.

I noticed my brow was wet with sweat. All the crew had been unnerved by the long battle with the weather and the hours of uncertainty. It was a great relief to be on the ground. We were safe. We had made it. The General had won his battle with the storm.

... I thanked the boss with all my heart as he climbed down from the plane onto the field.

Chapter 13

Physician to a World Diseased

The lights of Boston were just beginning to twinkle as we flew over. Our plane seemed almost motionless in its flight. We were flying on a steady south-southwest course directly to Washington D.C. Night was fast approaching.

Like small diamonds in the velvet shadows of the evening, lights sparkled from the rolling hills of New England. Villages and towns passed beneath our wings, breaking out like a rash of tiny fires in the gathering darkness.

We flew in over the sprawling suburban areas of New York. The headlights of cars streaming back and forth on the West Side Highway created a solid ribbon of whiteness in the night. There were thousands of them ... it was dazzling.

Downtown New York City was glowing with a milky haze. Graceful bridges spanning the East River and the Hudson shone proudly forth. Beneath them, a freighter glided on the ebb tide to the sea.

We had been lucky. The brilliant cities of America had not been touched by the hand of the war. Here we had no ugly ruins to clear away, no factories to rebuild. We had been spared all that.

To come from the horrors of war-torn Germany back to America was like travelling to another planet, a new world. Could those tortured ruins be only a few thousand miles away, those windowless hulks of buildings, those collapsed churches, those homes that were heaps of rubble, those people looking back with horror and looking forward without hope?

Would America understand? Would those people down there – driving those hundreds of cars – know what life had been like for us?

Or would we forget and live as selfishly as ever? We had lived riotously in the '20's. In the '30's we lived through a terrible depression ... then, once again, we prepared for war. In the '40's we paid the dreadful price. Many of my pals were gone forever, sacrificed on the altar of freedom, living and laughing only in eternal memory.

... Was the same cycle starting all over again?

We flew on over the plains and forests of New Jersey and Pennsylvania. Dimples of light winked at us from the occasional farmhouses like stars in the night.

"Mac," the navigator shouted, "What are you going to do when you hit the ground?"

"I don't know," I replied. "Got any ideas?"

"First of all, it's a snack bar and a big double-decker 'burger with relish, catsup, *everything* they can load on it, about five bottles of coke and a sundae. And then, MAN! What I *ain't* gonna' do!"

Soon we could see Washington from the cockpit window. The General came forward. The floodlit needle of the Washington Monument welcomed us from afar.

We were coming home. At last we were coming home.

We landed. As we brought the giant bomber down the taxi strip, I could see the lights of Washington over the terminal building. The Capitol was a dazzling white against the night. The Jefferson Memorial cast a perfect reflection in the still waters of the Tidal Basin.

"Man, what a lovely city! What a lovely city!" the navigator was saying.

We cut the fuel, switched off the ignition and the engines coughed to a stop. The warm balmy air of Washington was sweet with summer. I shoved open the window and drew a long breath. It was wonderful to be home again – *home* after so many months abroad.

Physician to a World Diseased

As I sat there looking out, I loved my country. I loved it more than I ever had before. I decided with all my heart that I would fight until my last breath to keep her great and strong and free.

... The next day, I rose early. While I was listening to God in the stillness of the morning, I wrote down these words:

Physician to a world diseased

Home again! Where years ago my fathers found a land
And made it home. Those cities – are they mine?
Unscathed by bombs? Those airfields –
Are there no blasted craters there?

Is this my land – untouched by war? Not bruised by might?
This country fair and free –
Why do I feel a stranger here?
Here are no wounds. Do I think that this should not be so?

Those industries I see as flying over them ... I think
Could they well be destroyed completely
As I saw in Frankfurt – bare?

Is this not home – the land I fought to see
Untouched by war and so, to free
A world diseased by passions of misguided men?
Where is my heart? I feel a pang of grief.
Is it not here – where cities proud and bright
Shine forth against God's starlit night?

Had I once thought in days gone by
That, once returned to Freedom's lair,
My mind would turn, sincere and true,
Not home – but rather back
To battlefields and flak-filled skies,
To peoples bombed yet fighting through,
To East London, Brussels, Paris too,
In heartfelt sympathy and love?

A Pathway through the Sky

This is my land – has it been true
To promises, so filled with words
Of 'free from fear, and want, and need'?
I have been 'home' where men's deeds, not words, held true.
His freedom and His love for life,
His hope of rebirth, free from strife,
A future, not of blood and death,
But happy, now, courageous, free

To build the world He longs to see.
This is my home. May she soon see
Her true responsibility.
Not words – but deeds sincere,
For hers the task to truly be
Physician to a world diseased.

May 14th, 1945

Chapter 14

A Light in the Sky

We had been out for a short swim in Bermuda during the afternoon, and I was still tingling with a sense of freshness and well-being. The sun was setting behind us, sinking slowly beneath the horizon of the sea. The stars were beginning to come out.

I was on one of my first long-distance hops across the Atlantic from the Pentagon. We were bound for Paris and London to pick up General Carl Spaatz and his staff and to fly them back across to Washington. General Spaatz, Commanding General of US Army Air Forces in Europe, would be greeted with a hero's welcome on his return.

Our B-17 Flying Fortress was comfortably and beautifully equipped for his convenience on the Atlantic crossing.

We took off from Bermuda that evening. About four hours flying time out, I switched off with the co-pilot at the controls and went back to stretch out for a rest. I was contented and at peace. There were almost no clouds and clear weather had been forecast all the way to Santa Maria Airport in the Azores, approximately five hours flying time ahead of us.

I fell soundly asleep. We droned on through the starry night, fast approaching the point of no return.

Suddenly, I was awakened. The plane was shaking violently. I got up with a start and flung off the covers. Quickly glancing at my watch, I dashed up to the cockpit.

"It's our Number Two," the co-pilot shouted. ... I stared out of the left window. Our inboard engine was vibrating crazily, threatening to shake the engine-mount to shreds.

"The magneto has gone out of timing!" the engineer shouted.

A Pathway through the Sky

"Feather it! Feather Number Two!" I yelled.

The pilot pressed frantically on the hydraulic control to Number Two. The propeller blades slowly turned into the wind.

"Cut it off!"

The propeller slowed down and stopped turning altogether. The vibrations ceased. I took my seat and increased the power to each of the three other engines.

We were four hours from the Azores. But our speed was cut back by about thirty miles an hour ... meaning we would be delayed for up to an hour. If anything happened to any of the other engines, we would have to go down and ditch the plane.

Suddenly, I remembered a thought that came to me in guidance a few days earlier: "On this next trip across the Atlantic, your faith will be tested."

Your faith will be tested? At the time, I didn't understand what that would mean and promptly put the thought out of my mind.

Our radio operator immediately got in contact with the station at the Azores and told them our situation. We alerted Coast Guard ships along our route as well.

The minutes passed slowly.

We had shut the fuel line to our Number Two engine and therefore had more gasoline in reserve for the other three engines. But because we had increased power to those engines, we were drawing nearly the same amount of fuel as would have been necessary to power all four.

An hour passed. Then one of us saw a strange light near the horizon. It was hanging a few degrees to our right, quite low in the sky. It looked like a plane.

A Light in the Sky

"See that, Mac?"

"Yes. What do you think it is?"

"I dunno'. It's hard to tell."

We studied it for a while. The light appeared to be moving ahead of us at a speed slightly slower than our own. We would eventually catch up with it if it continued on the same course.

"It's *some* kind of plane," I said. I asked the radio operator to try to make contact. The radio operator fiddled around with his knobs and controls. I could hear Morse Code signals and noisy atmospherics coming in on the receiver.

"I can't seem to reach him, sir," the radio officer reported.

We flew on. The light slowly rose higher above the horizon, almost imperceptibly.

The rest of the crew had taken interest in the light by now. Every eye was on it as we slowly closed the gap of distance that seemed to separate us.

"Looks like a C-54," the captain said presently.

I stared intently through the night.

"A C-54?" the navigator chuckled. "That would be a story for the folks back home. Imagine – a B-17 with one engine out, overtaking a C-54."

"They'd never believe it."

The crew was relaxing. The other plane had taken our minds off our worries for the moment.

Another half hour passed. The light rose higher and higher in the sky until it was nearly above us. It was brilliant yellow in color. We were studying it with increasing interest. The radio operator still was unable to make contact.

The flight engineer spoke up. "You know, I'm beginning to change my mind."

"So am I," I replied. It was a strange light ... there were no red and green wing-tip lights flashing on and off.

"What is it, then?" the radio operator inquired.

"Search me."

We flew on. The navigator was studying the light through his astrodome.

"What do you make of it?" I shouted down.

"Looks like a star ... or like one of the planets."

Suddenly, it occurred to me. We had been completely fooled. Flying eastwards through the night, in a direction opposite to the rotation of the earth, we had been 'catching up' on the panorama of stars overhead. We had mistaken one particularly bright star for a C-54.

When we realized our mistake, the whole crew roared with laughter. *This* was a story we'd never forget. Where did we learn aircraft identification anyway – at Mount Palomar?

We were in a good mood. I looked at my watch. We were only two hours and ten minutes out of the Azores. Our fuel supply was still ample.

I relaxed and praised God. The light had been a diversion. It had given us a sense of company and protection. For a while, we had been totally convinced that there was another aircraft in the sky ahead of us. It had brightened all our spirits.

A Light in the Sky

Just as dawn was breaking, we came down over the deep blue waters of the sea and made our approach into Santa Maria airport. A golden light was painting the mountain peaks of the Azores. ... We landed.

By early afternoon, our engine magneto was repaired. We continued on without mishap to Paris, and then back to Washington DC with General Spaatz and his staff.

This was the first of two times that God showed His infinite mercy and care by a source of light in the night.

... The second time came later that same summer of 1945.

CHAPTER 15

A Pathway through a Storm

It was late August, 1945. I was flying about four miles south of the small town of Grayling, Michigan, when we encountered the storm. Torrents of rain were pouring down, and turbulence threw my small AT-6 trainer about as though it were a small boat on a boiling sea.

I grew anxious. I had just enough fuel to fly on to St. Ignace, Michigan, 70 miles to the north ... but no further. If only we could make it through the storm and find the small grass strip.

The weather officer in Detroit had told me not to expect any bad weather. How had he made such a mistake?

I looked at my watch. 7:45 p.m. Another 20 minutes until sunset. Daylight was failing fast.

... That was another thing. There were no lights on the field at St. Ignace. At night, it would be impossible to see the runway. I needed every moment of time that was left before nightfall.

My only passenger, Sergeant Duncan Corcoran of the United States Army Air Corps, had been silent for several minutes.

"How are you doing back there, Duncan?" I asked.

"Okay, Jimmy, I'm doing fine!" I smiled when I heard his rich Scottish brogue. I sometimes found it hard to understand what Duncan was saying, but he was a cheerful companion to have along.

"How much longer will it be?" he shouted from the back cockpit.

"Oh, another 25 minutes. Maybe more because of this weather." I tried to sound more confident than I felt. Our little plane pitched and heaved in the violent gusts of wind. It was constantly getting darker.

We passed over Grayling and headed straight up the main

Pathway through a Storm

highway to the north. The heavy rain had cut visibility down to nil.

Fifteen minutes passed. We flew over the lights of Mackinac City, a small harbor city on the south shore of the Straits of Mackinac. It was almost pitch dark ahead.

"Not far now," Duncan shouted from the back.

"No." It *wasn't* far. But it was hard to know which way to go. I strained to see through the inky darkness.

There was a light! Far out across the water, I could make out a small light in the direction of St. Ignace. I headed for it. Perhaps it was a beacon on the far shore.

As we got closer to the light, my heart fell. It was a lone freighter, wending its passage through the straits between the two promontories of land. St. Ignace was not in sight.

I turned and headed back for Mackinac City. Circling over the lights of the small town, I picked out a few noticeable landmarks. Then I set out across the water a second time on an estimated heading to St. Ignace.

My landing lights cast a spray of whiteness into the rain. We plunged on through the darkness. We had only 15 minutes of fuel left in our tanks.

Suddenly, I had a picture in my mind's eye of a great light. The light was shining down on the field at St. Ignace, illumining a pathway from the sky. It was only a vision ... but something said in my heart, "This miracle will actually happen. Have no fear"

I flew on. Minutes later, there was St. Ignace ahead. Through openings in the clouds I could make out the lights of the town, spread along a curving bay. Little red neon lights were flashing on and off in front of drugstores and gas stations. Giant ferries, lit up like Christmas trees, were moored at the long railway piers.

A Pathway through the Sky

"Where's the field?" Duncan shouted from behind.

"It's somewhere north of the city – about three miles out of town," I shouted. Our plane was buffeting madly in the wind currents.

We flew on over the town and headed north. I searched and searched for the field. I could see nothing. It was pitch black.

... I turned back towards St. Ignace.

In the center of the town, I saw a tall radio tower, lit by winking red lights. I decided to circle the city. Perhaps I could draw some attention. If only *someone* could give us some help.

We had 13 minutes of fuel left.

My fingers fumbled with the knobs of the radio. Hadn't I remembered some Civil Aeronautics Authority station at the field? I tried to recall the frequency.

"This is Army 1705 calling St. Ignace radio. Army 1705 calling St. Ignace radio."

"St. Ignace radio to Army 1705. Go ahead, please."

I was tremendously relieved to hear a human voice. I quickly explained our situation. We were low on gas. We needed to land. Could he please give us some ...

"St. Ignace radio to Army 1705. I have no authority to give instructions to Army aircraft. Will get in touch with Army Control Detroit."

"But ..."

The radio was dead.

Army Control *Detroit?* It was ridiculous. This was no job for Army Control Detroit! What did he think he was doing?

We kept circling the town. I weighed our alternatives. If worse came to worst, we could go up into the clouds, and bail out. But if we came down in the Great Lakes, we'd never be found.

I was not afraid for my own safety by bailing out. But to endanger Sergeant Corcoran's life was a risk I did not want to take. He was older than I was. There was no telling how he would handle himself in a "jump" or how he would survive the cold.

There was another consideration. As a flying officer, operating out of the Pentagon, I had been given the small AT-6 for the purpose of maintaining my quotient of flying hours. To crash the plane and lose it would be a shameful disgrace – not to speak of the probability we would both be killed.

I was going to do everything I could think of to get the plane safely on the ground.

We flew on and on in a wide circle. Fear crept into my heart.

"Hello Army 1705. St. Ignace Radio to Army 1705."

Thank God!

"Army 1705 to St. Ignace radio. Come in."

"Army control advises you go to Lansing – repeat, advises you go to Lansing."

I felt my temper rising. We now had eight minutes of gasoline left. Lansing was a good hour and a half flying time away. Didn't he get the point?

"Look. We've got to land at this field. Lansing is out of the question. I can't see where the field is. It is pitch dark. Can you give me some idea of where we are and try to direct us in?"

The officer sounded startled. "Just a moment." ... Again the radio went dead.

A Pathway through the Sky

The wind was buffeting the plane with extraordinary violence. Our airspeed was over 170 miles an hour. I cut the throttles back a bit.

"St. Ignace radio to Army 1705. My microphone is twenty yards from the nearest door. It is impossible to locate you and give directions at the same time. By the time I get to the mike, you've flown on another mile or two."

... Seven minutes of gas left.

Suddenly, I had a thought. "Look, do you have a car at the field?"

"Yes – my own car."

"Well, get in your car and flash your headlights on and off. I'll be able to see that."

"All right," came the reply, "I'll park at the north end of the field."

"Good. Get a whole bunch of cars. Get them all out there blinking their headlights on the field."

"Wilco." The radio went dead again.

To my horror, I discovered that my airspeed was down to stalling speed. The plane was shuddering in the first stages of the stall. Quickly I shoved the throttle forward and the engine roared back to full power.

A wave of cold sweat swept over me. I was only a few feet above the tree-tops. I had come within inches of disaster by a simple incident of neglect. Never had I known a fear so strong, even in all my bombing missions over Germany. I felt the taste of death in my mouth.

Suddenly, I saw a long line of cars heading out the road that led north from the town. A police patrol car was at the head of the line. I saw its revolving dome light as it sped northward.

Pathway through a Storm

Where were those cars going? Surely it couldn't be to the airfield. There hadn't been time for the control officer to get a message into town. ... But there they were!

The line of cars turned in at a small road. Suddenly, the radio came alive again.

"St. Ignace radio to Army 1705. Can you see the car headlights near the field?"

Yes! Yes! They *were* going to the airfield.

"Yes, I can," I shouted, hoarse with excitement. "Tell them ... tell them to line up alongside the field. Place two cars at each end of the field with headlights facing towards the center – two along the sides to give the width."

"Wilco."

Sergeant Corcoran was sitting quietly in the back. I wondered if he knew how close we had come to disaster.

I banked around in a long curve. Rain was slashing down across the windshield and it was hard to see through the torrents of water pelting through the air.

The cars on the field moved around into position. I could now make out the outline of the small grass strip.

I checked the gas. Three minutes left. There was enough fuel to make one low pass over the field. I came in over the tree-tops and made a sweep across the grass strip, my landing lights illuminating the surface. I searched the field, making sure that there were no objects lying in the way. Then I climbed up into the night to make my final approach.

As I came in, I gazed down on the sight before me. My vision had come true! *The entire field was lit up.* Cars were parked on every side, their twin headlights shining out across the grass. Every square yard of the field was plainly visible from the air. The landing strip shone out from the darkness of the night.

That night, I made one of the best landings in my whole career as a pilot.

Chapter 16

September 1957 - Reflections

Tom Moore, the old retired fire chief of St. Ignace, rocked slowly back and forth in his chair.

"Yes, that was a night I will never forget," he was telling me. "I remember I was sitting outside the door at the town hall. The town council was meeting inside and I was waiting to lock up after they left. It was raining like cats and dogs – my arthritis was killing me.

"Suddenly, I heard your plane flying overhead in the dark. I thought to myself, 'It's no night for a fellow to be out in a plane.' I wondered what in the heck was wrong ... figured you were in trouble of some kind.

"As I was sitting there, God spoke to me very clearly. He told me, 'Go turn in the alarm.'

"I got up from where I was sitting, raced over and turned in the alarm. Then I ran out to get the driver of the fire-truck. We pulled out of the barn and headed north towards the airport at full speed.

"I passed the state police headquarters down the road. A couple of squad cars joined us there. Many folks drove up in their cars.

"'Get out to the airport,' I yelled. 'Get out to the airport as fast as you can!'

"Pretty soon, we had a long line of cars travelling north in that driving rain-storm. I didn't know what we were going to do when we got out to the airfield. I just knew we had to get out there and *fast!*

"When we got to the field, the radio operator told us to line up on both sides of the runway and to shine our headlights onto the field. The truck driver drove the fire-truck down to the end of the strip and the rest of the cars parked along the sides.

A Pathway through the Sky

"Then we all waited, and pretty soon, there you were. Everyone had climbed out of their cars and were standing in the rain watching.

"Then you came in for the second time. Everyone said it was the prettiest landing they had ever seen."

I stood on the stern of the Arnold Line ferryboat, *MV Huron,* watching as the shoreline of St. Ignace grew smaller in the distance. Our wake had smoothed a track across the ruffled surface of the waters, a track which curved around the old railroad pier and the small sheltered harbor we had left minutes before.

Over the rim of the low hills, I could make out the red tower of the police station I had flown around on that terrible stormy night in 1945. In the 12 years that had gone by since then, the old airfield had been abandoned and was now fully overgrown with grass and weeds.

To the south, there was a gigantic new landmark, graceful and magnificent. It was the new Mackinac Bridge, longest suspension span in the world at the time, connecting the northern and southern peninsulas of Michigan. At night, its lights shone forth in beautiful curving lines along the suspension cables and the roadway.

The ferry rolled in the gentle swell of the waves. I was lost in my thoughts and memories.

Twelve long and full years had passed since I was discharged from the Air Force. They had been wonderful years ...

My mind drifted back to the day when General Anderson had released me from active duty. We had talked together in his Pentagon office, chatting over old times.

The General listened intently to all my stories of the war - of the time I survived an almost inevitable ditching in the North Sea by heeding the Voice of God and obeying. I told him about the near-collision with another B-24 in the fog, and how we had come back

September 1957 - Reflections

with only one and a half minutes flying time left.

We reminisced about our trip into the heart of Germany just before the war ended – how we had flown at low-level over dozens of utterly devastated cities and towns and ruined industrial areas, driven by jeep into streets where the fighting was still going on, and visited damaged factories and concentration camps.

I told the General those five days had seared my soul and changed the direction of my life. They made me determined to find an answer to the root causes of war and hatred and division.

I told him of the life-changing experience I had in London in late 1944, meeting with the international team of Moral Re-Armament. I had sensed, even then, that I would find the avenue for my deepest aspirations within this work.

I asked the General if I might be released for active, full-time service with MRA. ... Like a father, he gave me every encouragement on the road I had chosen.

During the years that followed, I travelled around the world to many nations with task forces of Moral Re-Armament, gathered from every walk of life. They had been years of new responsibilities, years of sacrifice, years of the fulfillment of all my dreams.

―――

The shrill whistle of the ferry interrupted my thoughts. We were coming around the old stone breakwater and the lighthouse. I gazed at the small harbor of Mackinac Island ahead.

It was getting quite late in the autumn. The trees were mostly bare ... only a few rusty tattered leaves clung to the branches. The leaden grey of the sky looked cold enough to hold a snow flurry or two. Winter was not far away now.

It was getting late ... late in the world as well, I thought. It was time to take action, to be willing to go into combat again.

The challenge to every man and woman was to live their lives in obedience to God, and to fight to bring unity and peace to the world. We needed to fly through the flak again, through the storms, through the darkness, depending on the light of God's guidance to bring us through.

EPILOGUE

James A. McLaughry – 1924-2015
by Ann McLaughry Gronda

My father made the final landing of his life on June 30th, 2015, passing away peacefully at Johanna Shores Presbyterian Homes in Arden Hills, Minnesota. He was 91 years old, and had lived 70 long and full years after World War II.

The story of those 70 years began in late September 1945 when 21-year-old Jim was discharged from active duty with the U.S. Army Air Forces and released from his assignment as personal pilot and aide to General Frederick Anderson. He was awarded the Air Medal with three Oak Leaf Clusters and two European Battle Stars for his service.

Like so many returning WWII veterans, Jim had choices to make. He considered going back to college, working with his father in the tool manufacturing business, or even running for public office, a long-held dream.

Inspired by friends, he decided instead to commit his life to helping heal a war-torn world. He accepted an invitation to join in a global effort known then as Moral Re-Armament[1]. MRA's endeavors in the years after the war included drawing Japan and Germany back into the family of nations, laying foundations of trust and friendship between France and Germany, and rebuilding democratic society in Japan.

From 1945 to 1965, Jim served as a full-time volunteer for Moral Re-Armament, helping organize its world conferences and performing in its musical productions that travelled to 26 nations. Over time, a separate organization was formed called Up With People, for which he worked as pilot and aviation director.

---

[1] Known today as Initiatives of Change

During this period, Jim had noticed a lovely pianist in the group named Nancy Hawthorne, and finally worked up the courage to ask for her hand. The wedding took place in Stamford, Connecticut on August 22nd, 1967. The priest, Fred McCarthy, was one of Jim's closest buddies from the earliest days of flight training 24 years before.

Jim then began a new career as a corporate pilot, flying jet and turboprop aircraft. During this time and into retirement Jim was a loving father to me and later my husband Bob, and a beloved grandfather to our children Kirk and Faith. Jim and Nancy were treasured members of their communities in New Lenox and Rockford, Illinois and most recently Johanna Shores Presbyterian Homes in Minnesota.

Jim did hit the target he had aspired to. Beneath the stories of God's visible presence in our lives, his actions displayed a deep love for people and a serving, selfless heart. These qualities endured, even when in later years he was faced with health-related challenges. At his funeral, Jim was described as an intentional listener, and as someone who was funny, but never joked at the expense of someone else. He stayed persistently engaged in life from the beginning until the very end, and will be sorely missed.

AFTERWORD

Background Information
by David Allen

In the summer of 1958, Jim McLaughry invited me to sit down and listen to his tapes and to read his notes and diaries about his experiences in World War II. He asked me to help him turn this material into a book.

I was honored that he would ask me to help preserve his memories. I was only 18 years old at the time, with almost no experience writing. We decided to write the book in the "first person" narrative. My challenge was to try to imagine myself as a B-24 Liberator bomber pilot, and, using Jim's notes and tape-recordings, to tell the story of his experiences in those war years.

Working together over that summer, we brought life and reality to his harrowing stories of survival and faith in the darkest hours of World War II. The result was the very first manuscript of "A Pathway through the Sky", the book you hold in your hands.

For one reason or another, we laid the manuscript aside for 55 years – and only in the spring of 2013 did we decide to bring it back to life. Jim called me with an urgent request that I recover the old typewritten copies of our first draft and convert them to digital form, and then to edit and improve the text.

Jim still wanted to tell his story, to get it out to more people than his own family and friends. He believed his experiences had relevance to the deeply troubled world we live in today, a time when, more than ever, he felt we need the hand of God to help us through the darkening skies of our age.

We spent many months reworking the text and drafting the story of the seven decades of his life after the war. I am gratified that Jim lived long enough to see this book put in final form.

As I set to work bringing our 1958 manuscript back to life, I delved deeply into the historical records of the 8th Air Force, the 392nd Bombardment Group and the 576th Bombardment Squadron. I read extensively about the air war in Europe and researched records on the career of Major General Fredrick L. Anderson, Jim's "boss" in the last months of the war. I read Jim's own diary of the seven-day trip he took over bombed-out Germany with General Anderson in April 1945. I learned so much more than I knew or understood in 1958 when we were composing the first draft of the book.

There are several stories worth telling from my research.

When Jim McLaughry and his B-24 Liberator bomber crew arrived in England in late June, 1944, the United States Eighth Air Force had reached its peak manpower strength of more than 200,000. With 40 heavy bomber groups, 15 fighter groups and four specialized support groups, it was the largest of the U.S. Army Air Forces deployed in combat anywhere during World War II.

As the USAAF's first "strategic" air force, its primary mission was to cripple and destroy Germany's war-making power through long-range daylight bombing operations in Western Europe. Following the D-Day landings, it also had a limited tactical mission of supporting the advancing Allied armies.

The final months of World War II were some of the deadliest for the US Army Air Forces in Europe ... and Jim's crew would be thrown into the worst of it.

They were assigned to the 392nd Bombardment Group, based at the former Royal Air Force base at Wendling in the heart of rural Norfolk in East Anglia. From August through December, 1944, Jim made 24 sorties into combat as part of the 576th Bombardment Squadron. He was credited with 21 missions. As he relates in this book, he and his crew came back 14 times either with wounded aboard, flying home on fewer than four engines, or his aircraft

Afterword

crippled with mechanical failure due to enemy action.

Their missions took them deep into the heart of Germany ... to a Mercedes-Benz aircraft engine plant on the outskirts of Stuttgart, to an ordnance manufacturing depot in Hannover, to a big oil refinery complex on the outskirts of Hamburg, to a Heinkel aircraft factory near the outskirts of Berlin, to marshalling yards near Wiesbaden on the Rhine ...

These missions carried a terrible price. Scores of aircraft went down in flames due to intensive and often highly accurate flak attacks in the region of the targets. Luftwaffe fighter attacks were responsible for other terrible losses. Downed aircrews were either killed or captured as prisoners of war.

Half of the U.S. Army Air Force's casualties in World War II were suffered by Eighth Air Force. Over the course of the war, Jim's bombardment group, the 392nd, would fly 285 combat missions, and suffer 1,552 casualties with 835 killed in action or in the line of duty. 184 aircraft were lost between September 9th, 1943 and April 25th, 1945.

Jim vividly describes in this book the horrifying experiences he went through. Several times he saw planes falling through the skies trailing smoke or exploding in the air; he witnessed whole crews dying in combat. His own life was in danger over and over again.

It took incredible courage and sacrifice for Jim and his crew to return to targets deep inside Germany day after day - to fly back again and again into those skies of fire and death. Focused on performing their mission and simply trying to keep themselves alive, they were only dimly aware of the destruction they were unleashing on cities, towns, and industrial areas below them.

Most aircrews never saw war-time Germany except from 25,000 feet – or from the inside of a German prison camp. They could have little concept of the ruin, damage and devastation below their wings.

A Pathway through the Sky

But, everything was about to change for Jim McLaughry in early 1945. He was soon to see Germany's appalling devastation at first hand. Through a remarkable turn of events, Jim was selected to become the personal pilot for Major General Frederick L. Anderson, Jr., the Deputy Commander for Operations, United States Strategic and Tactical Air Forces (USSTAF).

Jim was totally taken by surprise when his orders came down on March 12th 1945. Not only had he never heard of General Anderson. As Jim told his commanding officer, "I've never even *seen* a general before!" He was quickly to learn who his new boss was ...

Throughout 1943, General Anderson had been the Commanding General of the VIII Bomber Command, based in England. He had been responsible on a daily basis for assigning bombing targets in Western Europe to heavy bombardment groups. He was involved in making some of the most dramatic and courageous command decisions in the air war in Europe, notably the long-distance coordinated strike on the Messerschmitt factories at Regensburg and the ball-bearing plant at Schweinfurt in August, 1943.

In February 1944, Major-General Anderson catapulted to the highest ranks of the command structure. There had been a massive reorganization of American airpower in Europe. The VIII Bomber, Fighter and Air Support Commands were combined into the United States Eighth Air Force with Major General Jimmy Doolittle as commanding general. The Eighth, Ninth and Fifteenth Air Forces were brought under control of a centralized headquarters for command of all US Army Air Forces in Europe, the United States Strategic and Tactical Air Forces (USSTAF).

General Anderson was appointed Deputy Commander for Operations for USSTAF under General Carl Spaatz, and was placed in charge of coordinating the operations of the 8th Air Force in Britain, and the 15th Air Force in the Mediterranean. In the last two months of World War II in Europe, Anderson was also responsible for assessing the accuracy and effectiveness of the strategic bombing missions he had sent out over Western Europe in 1943 and 1944.

Afterword

When Jim reported for duty at the European headquarters of USSTAF in mid- March, 1945, he was struggling to believe the sudden changes in his life ... "One day, a co-pilot on a bomber crew; the next day, the personal pilot to a general." As he writes, he was awed at first by the General's rank and position, but soon found that Anderson began to treat him as a fellow pilot and a friend.

Over several weeks Jim was entrusted with increasing administrative duties and gradually became more than just the General's personal pilot. He became a trusted aide-de-camp to the General and, on occasion, his armed bodyguard.

Between April 17th and 22nd, 1945, Jim piloted General Anderson into the heart of Germany to assess the effectiveness of the various strategic bombing missions Anderson had been responsible for sending over Europe. They flew at low-level over thirty cities, towns and factories; they drove by jeep into cities where fighting was still going on; they visited damaged factories and concentration camps.

Those five days were to sear Jim's soul. His diary of those five days was titled "A Trip through a Land of the Dead". He describes flying over Frankfurt: "city completely in shambles ... not one house unaffected". Flying over Schweinfurt: "city and factories well blasted", "no bridges intact". Flying over Mannheim and Ludwigshafen: "crashed ME 109's and wounded barges on the river", "industries knocked out". Flying on to Hanau: "there is no town there at all, completely wiped out". Flying on to Leipzig: "fighting still going on. ... many fires in city ... the city itself pretty well crumbled." Driving into Nuremberg: "City completely in rubble. This beautiful historic city – what a mess. ... Just riding through deadens me – what must living here be like? What hope is there for these people?"

To the great industrial centers of the Ruhr: Dortmund, Krefeld, Essen, Dusseldorf, Wuppertal, and Solingen - "... the ruined Ruhr ... bomb craters wherever you look." To Cologne: "historic old cathedral still standing ... no other building remains intact over fifteen feet from ground level".

A Pathway through the Sky

On April 22nd, Jim drove into Weimar looking for a length of hose to siphon gas into his Beech aircraft from the C-47. What he saw that day horrified him; "... came upon the killing factory near Buchenwald ... gas chambers looked like shower rooms from inside and like a ten-car garage from outside ... then went over to the concentration camp ... saw some of the incinerators and were shown where the dead had been piled – the smell of death was all around."

In his diary, he wrote, "... Even after having seen and heard all the sounds of the agony of many humans, it is hard for me to believe what I've seen and heard."

After the war, Jim McLaughry spent 20 years of his life working without pay for Moral Re-Armament (MRA) - and subsequently for its offshoot, Up With People. In the first years after World War II, Moral Re-Armament was credited by many sources for its successful efforts to draw Japan and Germany back into the family of nations, to laying the foundations of trust and friendship between France and Germany, to turning back the tide of Communist influence in the coal mines and trade unions of Germany and Italy, and to rebuilding the institutions of democratic society in Japan.

For those interested in learning more about the work of Moral Re-Armament after World War II, I would recommend "Franco-German Reconciliation: The Overlooked Role of the Moral Re-Armament Movement" by Edward Luttwak in *Religion, the Missing Dimension of Statecraft*, Douglas Johnston and Cynthia Sampson (editors), Oxford University Press 1994.

THE LORD IS MY KEEPER

... Through the worst hours of combat and throughout his long life, Jim has been comforted and restored by the words of his favorite Psalm – the 121st.

I will lift up mine eyes unto the hills,
    from whence cometh my help.
My help cometh from the LORD,
    which made heaven and earth.
He will not suffer thy foot to be moved:
    He that keepeth thee will not slumber
Behold, He that keepeth Israel
    shall neither slumber nor sleep.
The LORD is thy keeper:
    the LORD is thy shade upon thy right hand.
The sun shall not smite thee by day,
    nor the moon by night.
The LORD shall preserve thee from all evil:
    he shall preserve thy soul
The LORD shall preserve thy going out and thy coming in
    from this time forth, and even for evermore.

***The Holy Bible*: King James Version 2000**

Made in the USA
Monee, IL
27 May 2021